Career Search: Are You on the Right Path?

By Larry A. Shepard

"Career Search: Are You On the Right Path?," by Larry A. Shepard. ISBN 978-1-60264-439-7.

Published 2009 by Virtualbookworm.com Publishing Inc., P.O. Box 9949, College Station, TX 77842, US. ©2009, Larry A. Shepard. All rights reserved. No part of this publication may be reproduced, stored in a retrieval system, or transmitted in any form or by any means, electronic, mechanical, recording or otherwise, without the prior written permission of Larry A. Shepard.

Manufactured in the United States of America.

CONTENTS

SHAKING UP THE COMFORT ZONE 1
MISSION AND VISION STATEMENTS 34
SPIRITUAL 42
FINANCIAL 47
RESUMES 59
NETWORKING 92
USING THE INTERNET & RECRUITERS 108
INTERVIEWING 117
ENTREPRENEURSHIP 144
GOAL SETTING 149
JOB ACCEPTANCE 158
PUTTING IT ALL TOGETHER 166
HAVE YOU… 179
INDEX 181

1.
SHAKING UP THE COMFORT ZONE

DOWNSIZING, RIGHTSIZING, OUTSOURCING, MERGERS, BUYOUTS, AND restructures. These are words that can make a grown man cry. These are certainly not words that brought a smile to your face as you cleaned out your desk. However, you must look at it in a sense that the sun always comes out after a storm. Certainly this is a life changing event but remember the old saying about making lemonade with a lemon. Have a good cry and then take a day or two to pull it together. Get over the anger and realize that this valley of despair is only temporary. After the anger you must hit the street running, hard and fast. With ever increasing global competition, outsourcing has dramatically increased over the last ten years. More companies realize that they can increase profits by paying lower wages through outsourcing their jobs to such areas as India and the Philippines. You may feel this is not the best way to do business and that American corporations should keep their resources within the country but that is a decision that we cannot make. These companies are governed by a board of directors more concerned about increased profits.

    The intent of this book is to offer you some guidance as you pursue this new phase in your life. Having gone through several cases of downsizing, I have had the opportunity to not only see what works for myself but many of my peers as well. I have developed my own strategies through observation plus trial and error. Not every one of them will work for you. I am a firm believer that you must implement most of the strategies in this book. You will find the right source that works for you but many times you may not realize what works until after you have tried it. What you thought might be the best method is only just another source to use. The ideas and thoughts in this book are but a compilation of the many contacts I have made thru my periods of transition and networking. These ideas came about from seeing what others have gone through and what worked for them. I networked extensively, attending meetings where I would not only develop a stronghold of contacts and ideas but also to assemble ideas that would help others in their search. I found that the more I assisted others, the more they helped me out.

Upon losing a job, there comes a disruption of the comfort zone. While we are employed we seldom think about being out of work. We are comfortable with our life and don't expect upheavals. We do not network nor are we on the lookout for other opportunities unless our current job is not satisfying us. It appears that the people who are more at a loss are those that are satisfied in their current jobs and believe that nothing will shake up their world. They do not look for other opportunities nor do they think that there is any chance they will lose their job. Most people do not prepare for these rainy days. They continue to charge heavy on credit cards and carry high mortgage payments. Their dedication to the so called "good life" is the basis of their trying to keep up with the Jones. Too often these people feel that as long as there is income then there is no need to worry about their rising debt. We will look into the financial aspect of being unemployed in a later chapter.

What must stand out is your faith that good will come of this tragedy. You cannot just sit back and wait for a job to come to you. One of my former networking friends stated that upon losing his job he waited two months for one to come along. He failed to send out any resumes, enlist a recruiter or do any networking because he felt his qualifications would get him a job. Finally, one day he realized that no one was going to ring his doorbell with a new position. Remember the adage that God helps those who help themselves? You must develop a plan and stay motivated. It is the intention of this book to assist you in targeting your job search strategy not to offer any miracle advice. Your job search is not going to come to an end overnight. Many career consultants feel that 6 months or longer is common at the mid to senior manager level. You must also consider that it could take longer, perhaps up to one year. I have had friends that exceeded a year in their search. There were many instances I saw where the individual was in their job search well over a year and up to two years. Even though they did everything right, the job market just did not produce what they were looking for. With the 2008 recession, the job market changed drastically with unemployment hitting over 9% nationally, and in some metropolitan areas, over 9%.

Your mental attitude will play a tremendous part in obtaining a new position or directing your career search in a totally different direction. In 2008 it was finally accepted we were in a recession and jobs become even scarcer than prior to the recession, which means the effort needed to secure a new one must be even greater. The recession won't last forever but you cannot afford to wait and see. Not only must you work harder but smarter as well. You have to make every step count. Floundering is not an option. You must challenge yourself on a daily basis.

As you become more acclimated to the job search and develop a positive attitude, sit back and visualize in your mind the job that you really want and then imagine getting it. Don't just stop there but develop an in depth vision of not only attaining it, but set some goals once you receive it so that you will progress and perhaps set yourself up to avoid a future job loss. Picture everything about the job, such as the type of people you are working with and even what type of boss you will have. Of course, don't be disappointed if you do not get exactly what you want. But as you picture this new job you will develop more confidence in your job search.

We all have a tendency to jump right into our job search and spend all of our time seeking that position. What we forget is that not only do we need to be in a good frame of mind but we also must maintain or in many cases improve our health. The job search is stressful and that alone creates negative repercussions. Many people get so depressed that they resort to alcohol. This is a major mistake, not only to our wallet but to our health. Having one martini at home after a hard day job searching will not be your downfall, but losing count on the number of martinis you have is taking a step into quicksand. Too often have individuals developed a problem with alcohol and not only did it negatively affect their job search but their family life as well. Financial discourse is the number one reason for divorces.

Make sure you maintain a solid regiment of exercise, whether it is at a gym, YMCA or just at home. Obesity will soak up any energy that you have and we all know that you will need every bit of energy that you can muster to continue your job search. Diabetes has become a major disease, in large part caused by overweight. Perhaps you did not have an exercise routine prior to losing your job so this is a good time to get started. You can build time into your day without any valid excuses or interruptions. Most likely you will be home while the family is at work, school or their extracurricular activities. Take advantage of this quiet time. If you live in a housing subdivision perhaps your homeowners association provides some fitness equipment in the clubhouse. This is a wonderful time to take a negative situation and create a positive life changing experience. You cannot overlook the physical side of the job search. Stress increases during a career transition and it is important that you take the necessary time to take care of your body. Stress will have an effect on your sleep patterns. You may feel depressed during this period and that is when physical ailments become more common. Listen to what your body is telling you. If you feel tired and run down, stop and rest. Putting off the job search for a day or two is not going to doom you. Obviously you are going to have days when everything seems to go right and your energy level is at its maximum. Take advantage of these times and become more intense in your search. And make this a daily routine, not just when you think you have some spare time.

    The business world has changed drastically over the last 20 years and continues to do so. Back in the 1980's there was more loyalty, both on the part of the employee and the employer. Those times may never return. What each employee must do now is to always be mindful of what is happening within his or her respective organization. You must watch for indications of downsizing, restructuring, etc. Some things that may give you an indication are an increase in management meetings. Has there been a shakeup of top management? Are there signs of hostility from senior management? Do you see your supervisor spending more time in these meetings or with their supervisor? Do you normally attend staff or training meetings that are now non-existent or have you been left off the agenda? Do you see unfamiliar faces walking around? These could be executives doing their due diligence and sizing up the company to buy it or perhaps they are management consultants who have been brought in to look for excessive or unnecessary expenditures.

You might even see items in your local newspaper stating your company is having financial problems or perhaps even potential filings of bankruptcy. Bankruptcy does not always mean the company is going to close but it certainly means there will be some form of restructuring. Do you feel pressure to quit? There have been instances where a company puts additional added pressure on the employee, anticipating the employee may resign thus helping the company to avoid paying severance packages. This also may be indicated in undeserved poor performance reviews and failure to receive justified salary increases. Has there been a tendency to consolidate departments? I worked for one company that brought in a new president and he made it known he was going to eliminate some positions. In addition, he unfairly wrote up poor performance evaluations and failed to even look at the employee's comments about their plan for improvement. It became obvious that he was hoping these employees would leave on their own and not have to be terminated. Eventually, he eliminated two levels of senior management positions and replaced them by titling them with a different name and bringing in replacements who had worked for him in the past. Obviously this was not the fairest of situations but he had the full backing of the Board of Directors. Eventually, the company floundered and was sold.

These are only a few indications that there may be something brewing. By all means, this does not mean that if you should see any of the above that you should immediately resign. Keep in mind that it may not affect your department at all, or if it does there may be other positions within the organization you would qualify for and perhaps with more responsibility or an increase in wages. If you do see solid indication that your position may be eliminated, then start thinking about some financial protection, such as obtaining a home equity line of credit, called a HELOC. This will offer you some financial backup should your position be eliminated. Most banks offer these and do not charge closing costs other than the real estate appraisal. If you do not use the line of credit, you will not incur any interest expenses. With banks now tightening up on lending restrictions, it may be more difficult to obtain any source of financing if you are out of work.

And make it a point to get a current copy of your credit report to check to make sure there are no errors. Many hiring companies now pull credit reports and if there is something derogatory in the credit report, this could hinder a job offer. You are entitled to a free credit report once per year from any of the three reporting agencies. The free report will not give you the credit score but the more essential part is ensuring there is no unfounded derogatory information. Also, you need to check into the company's severance package and determine if the company has agreed to offer outplacement services. Many companies will provide services such as through DBM (Drake Beam Morin) that will assist you in your job search. These services are usually fully paid for by the company and free to you. Take advantage if they are offered.

Make sure you maintain a satisfactory relationship with your supervisor and their boss. Obviously being in good graces with your boss may prove beneficial at a later time. Going one level above may further enforce your status and there also may be the possibility that due to downsizing your boss may fall victim to it and leave you open for future possibilities should the company complete a turn around. Don't ever think that your business field will not suffer the consequences of downsizing. Most industries, such as banking and financial, pharmaceutical, manufacturing and home building have had their share. During the later part of 2006, all of 2007 and 2008 and well into 2009, the mortgage business went thru some tremendous downsizing due to the downturn of the housing market. The housing market went through five years of phenomenal sales so the bubble was sure to burst eventually. Many mortgage companies closed down, putting thousands of people out of work. The downturn of the housing market affected many professions such as mortgage brokers, realtors, construction trades, swimming pool companies, banks and major building supply companies such as Home Depot and Lowes.

One other thing you need to entertain just before leaving your current employer is to make sure you have reviewed your Outlook contacts page and copy down any contacts that could prove beneficial to your job search. You will not have access to this once your position is eliminated and often at the time you are in your supervisor's office getting the bad news, your computer access has been terminated and your desk has been cleaned out by security. Also, attempt to get a letter of recommendation from any of the supervisors you worked for. They will be more acceptable at this time to provide you with one to ease their consciences. This will assist in your future job search. In fact, if there are any sources in the company other than your supervisor, approach them for letters of recommendation also. You may find it more difficult to get them at a later time.

Should you fall victim to any source of termination, review your severance package to see what is available to you and what to expect. This also may be a negotiating tool. Perhaps, because of your service to the organization, the package could be increased. You may be able to negotiate additional benefits such as the company extending your medical coverage, at the same time picking up the cost of it. On one occasion I was downsized on the 15th of the month and the company agreed to keep my medical insurance in place until the 15th of the following month at which time the severance package kicked in. That not only gave me an additional month of salary but also eliminated the cost of medical insurance. Look into the possibility that your company will pay for additional job training to move you into another field. Many companies have job and training assistance but do not push it. Most companies do not have rigid standards for severance packages so that works in your favor.

COBRA is an acronym for the Consolidated Omnibus Budget Reconciliation Act, which was passed by Congress in 1986. It gives former employees, as well as retirees, the opportunity to continue their medical coverage at group rates. Unfortunately, it does not state that the company where you were employed has to pay any additional fees as they had done during your employment. You are now required to pay the entire cost of the plan yourself for the allowable 18-month duration. But keep in mind that this allows you to have one less worry. In many cases, just the monthly cost of prescriptions a family of five may use could be more than the cost of the COBRA. And if you were to purchase this coverage outside of a group plan, the cost could be considerably higher than COBRA. Keep in mind that your employer must notify you within 30 days of termination and you are eligible to continue the coverage in almost all cases. Termination for gross misconduct is one area you may not be eligible. The coverage would begin on the date the previous coverage terminated. The benefits would be exactly the same as the prior plan. COBRA may not be the most cost effective plan available but don't lose out on the opportunity to get it. Sign up for it and then search for a better plan. You cannot afford to not have any health insurance, especially if you have a family. Having a lapse in insurance coverage, especially if there are pre-existing conditions, may make it harder to get new coverage. There is a website, www.dol.gov, where you can get further information on COBRA. Make sure that you receive a Certification of Coverage from your current group insurance company. This verifies that you had insurance and will prevent any pre-existing conditions being eliminated from your coverage.

Upon termination the first thing you should do is to contact your local unemployment office immediately, in order to initiate an unemployment compensation claim. Most times this can be done electronically and you should not be hasty in the opening of the claim. In most cases you would be eligible for benefits. Never assume you are not eligible. It is imperative you contact the office and let them make the determination. Although the amounts are not equivalent to your prior earnings, it does provide you some relief during your period of unemployment. Make sure you keep records of the entire process, as you will be required to keep records of what attempts you made to find suitable employment. If you fail to look for a new position per the guidelines set, you could find yourself without any financial assistance from the unemployment office. Your claim would be cancelled and of course that eliminates those funds. Make sure you get a copy of the guidelines from the local unemployment office and review them. Do not be embarrassed to file this claim.

This is a benefit you are entitled to. Take advantage of it. Your former employer paid taxes to provide this benefit.

Let's go back to when you lost your job. You cannot let rage and anger set in. This will hinder any attempts you make in securing a new job, as it will show in your demeanor. Keep in mind what you do have and that you have others counting on you. Sit down with your family and talk it out. They will understand and perhaps have some good suggestions that will benefit your search. You have to get over being terminated. Check your ego at the door. If not, you face the possibility of bringing your family down and you need them to be there to support your efforts. Have yourself a good cry but then get down to business. Being out of work does not give you a license to sleep in and pull the bed covers up over your head. Get up and get dressed as if you were going to work and make it the same time you normally got up as when you were employed. This eliminates any opportunity to create a new habit. It will be tempting at times to stay in your pajamas but you must realize that looking for a new job is as much, if not more work than your previous work assignment.

You need to exercise every competitive advantage possible. This does not mean that you should repress your feelings. You have earned the right to let some pressure off. Just keep it behind closed doors. Your attitude must reflect the most positive appearance that is possible. Think that this is a new opportunity and even better blessings will confront you. Once you realize that you will not be retiring from this company, then it is time to create a plan. Be aware that many states are "employment at will" states where the employer can terminate you without reason, assuming it is not due to discrimination or sexual harassment. Although the Federal Equal Employment Opportunity laws (EEO) do not permit discrimination based on age, we all know it happens. It is very difficult to prove but be conscious of it. Being a baby boomer, I am well aware of it on a personal level. There are many cases where younger interviewers have a tendency to feel intimidated by older workers. Make it a point to put a positive spin emphasizing your experience and wisdom. During one of my interviews, upon walking into the room to meet the hiring manager, a gentleman in his early thirties, it was obvious right from the start that he had no interest in interviewing me. During our forty minute interview, he looked at his watch no less than six times and appeared bored just asking me questions. He failed to return any of my phone calls and on one occasion when I attempted to reach him on his office phone and left a message to call me back. Several hours late I attempted to reach him on his cell phone but I did not leave a message. Minutes later my cell phone ran and when I answered it stating my name there was a pause on the other end and then a hang up. When I researched the number, I found it was his cell phone. At that point I knew I was not in the running and I felt confident it had nothing to do with my qualifications or how I was dressed. One other point here is that whenever you leave an employer, do not burn any bridges. You never know when they may call you back.

The first stage of the plan is to create a team to assist you. You want 3 or 4 members who will support your efforts but at the same time they will be honest with you. These members should be willing to let you know your plan needs work or your efforts are not up to your capabilities. They must be there when you become frustrated and offer cheers for your efforts as well. Remember, not every day is going to produce good results. The team can consist of family members, friends, or former co-workers. It may include your Pastor or financial planner. Periodically, preferably weekly, you should sit down with each of them and indicate what your efforts were and the results those efforts produced. It is not necessary to bring all of them together. They may have suggestions how you could have been more productive. You cannot take it personally…they are there to help.

Once you have the initial meeting with your family, make sure you advise them of the direction in which you are going. Ensure that when they take telephone messages that these messages are clear with all the proper contact information. There is nothing more frustrating than getting a message about a potential interview and the family member has taken down the wrong phone number. They should get the callers name, company represented, phone number and best time for you to call back. Also make sure that voice messages are not deleted until you have heard them and returned the call. On the subject of voice messages, make sure your home voice mail message is appropriate. It should be professional and not recorded by your 5 year old child. This all falls along that first impression concept. Too often in my career I have called homes and felt embarrassed just listening to their message. If I was making the call to set up a candidate for an interview, I quickly removed them from consideration.

Always check your voicemail messages throughout the day if you are away from home. It could be vital you return their call immediately or perhaps it is a company that is in the neighborhood of where you will be that day. A recruiter will not make many attempts to reach you. They will just move on to the next candidate. Make sure there is a pen and paper next to the telephone at all times. This may be a time where you advise young children not to answer the phone. I have heard of cases where the young child answers the phone and if the calling party asks for Mr. or Mrs. and they are not there at that time, the child does not forward the call to the spouse. Explain it to your child and advise them this will change when you land your new job.

You are going to experience some high and low attitudes. Make every attempt to avoid the lows. A low attitude will show in your voice when you are speaking with potential employers. If you have to put a smiley face on the telephone as a reminder, then do so. You have to eliminate as much of the chaos that comes with the job search as possible. Being unemployed can wreck havoc on a family and its finances. It can also cut deeply, causing pain as well as wounded confidence and self esteem. During these low times, visit your Pastor and get some spiritual guidance. Make sure that prayer is a daily part of your life, not only while you are out of work, but upon receiving a position as well. Certainly you will have reason to offer praise when that right job comes along. Depression has a tendency to hit you during this period of unemployment. Some symptoms of depression come in the following: low self esteem or drop in confidence, loss or gaining of weight, lack of any energy, poor sleep habits, increase in the consumption of alcoholic beverages, and a change in eating habits such an increase in food intake or lack of eating. It can escalate to a more serious state of thoughts of suicide. Depression mainly occurs due to a feeling of not being able to do anything about your job loss; a feeling of helplessness. Should you see any of these symptoms seek professional help immediately.

Along with a "management team" establish a mentor. This can be anybody, but preferably someone who has gone through unemployment in the past, as they will prove to be an excellent source. They know what you are facing because they were there. Once you develop a mentor, have them review your resume. Meet with them weekly for a coffee as well and let them be part of developing your job search, but don't monopolize their time. Don't forget to send them a thank you. You will find this tool to be invaluable down the road. The mentor serves as a sounding board. Accept their input and be open to criticism of your plan and efforts. Remember they are there to help and look for opportunities to assist them if they are unemployed or looking to advance their career. And don't forget them when you do land by keeping in touch with them. You never know if you will need them again or maybe you will be able to help them down the road. Just keep in mind that this may not be your last time to be out of work. It is becoming too common to go through eight or ten job changes in your career. And it does not get any easier as you go, although you will become more adept at career searches.

Continuing or starting a fitness routine is vital to your well-being. If you feel good, you will be more productive. This does not necessarily mean you have to spend the money going to a gym. Start walking in the morning before you head out and after dinner. There are many good books in your local library that offer exercise plans without having to purchase expensive equipment. Just look in your garage and I am quite sure you will find several items that can serve as weights. A partially filled gallon paint can is one that comes to mind. You also do not need a treadmill to walk. Obviously there will be days due to inclement weather that walking will not be possible. Work your plan around this and have backup exercises. If you live in the northeast and it is in the middle of winter you are more restricted by the weather but refer to the exercises that can be done inside without the equipment.

Don't stop your hobbies because you are out of work, unless they require funds. If you are an avid golfer obviously you must curtail this due to the expense. But take up another hobby. Take your child or spouse's bicycle for a ride. Your children may enjoy the company and it will take your mind off the job search. There will be a tendency to feel guilty when you are enjoying your hobby but avoid this. You will need an outlet for any frustration that builds up. Look for hobbies that involve the entire family. They will need the outlet as well. Your spouse may be there with a wide grin on their face when you come home at night but inside they are worried about you. Help them with their pain as well.

Eating right is part of the fitness routine. Don't avoid meals and certainly watch out for snacking. If you are sitting there in front of the computer there will be a tendency to want to snack. Focus on the job search. If you eat right and continually maintain a personal fitness plan this will help your confidence. Unemployment is frightening and you need to offset the low days with as much positive thinking as possible. Rise early every day just like you were going to go to work. This is an ideal time to go for a walk and clear the cobwebs out of your head. It is also an excellent time to plan your day or plan what you will say during some of your visitations that day. There will be times you don't want to get out of bed and just want to pull the covers over your head. When you do this you are signaling your family that you are giving up. This is not what you want for yourself or them. This leads to further problems, from financial to physical to mental.

During the first couple of days after you have left your previous employer, it is a crucial time to develop a plan. Spend the time putting a plan together and then meeting with your mentor and management team. Remember that looking for a job is a job. You are definitely the President and CEO of your new company…You, Inc. Do you think that General Electric, Dell Computers or Kmart operate without a plan? Of course not and neither should you. You first may want to do an assessment of your skills and qualifications. Perhaps you were not even happy in your former profession. Maybe this act of termination is a blessing in disguise. This plan will enable you to focus your job search more efficiently and productively. This is also a good time to review your work experience as well as performance. Were you performing as well as you could have? Did your performance have anything to do with the downsizing? Is your current career best for you and are you changing with the times? Were you earning enough? Maybe you were underpaid for what you contributed at your previous company. Look at your skills and determine if they are up to date. Do you need additional education or certifications?

This may be an appropriate time to do an assessment of your skills and qualifications. You may realize you have more to offer a company or perhaps once you complete the assessment, it may be obvious that you are in the wrong field. Princeton Review offers an assessment test on the web. Go to www.review.com/career and take the assessment, but keep in mind any assessment should not be used to make your decisions but to give you data to use in your decision making process. Being unemployed will give you an excellent opportunity to find out who you really are. Learn who you are. What is inside of you? What fuels your professional career? What are your skills and how do they play into what you want to do? Is your education current and in line with what you want to do? What do you enjoy and do your hobbies and outside interests have any bearing on what your career path is? Do all of your values align with the direction of your career? These all need to be analyzed as you assemble a plan for your career search. If you have not burned any bridges at your last employer, go back and sit down with your former supervisor and get their honest opinion of your skills. They may be brutally honest, but necessary.

This is a good time to assess whether your skills are up to date, especially if you are in the IT world. Consider going back to school and taking some courses that will enhance your knowledge. Your industry most likely has changed considerably over just the last 5 years with the changes in the economy. Obtaining additional certificates or advanced degrees will say a lot when discussed during an interview. You can take online courses that will fit into your schedule at your convenience. Go back to your alma mater and see what they have to offer. This is the best place to start.

In the next chapter we will look into Mission and Vision Statements. These are an important part of your plan and actually one of the defined steps in your career search. The assessment you complete on yourself will assist you in developing both the Mission and the Vision Statements. Do not be reluctant or procrastinate in completing a plan. And on the other hand, don't rush it. It must be detailed and specific as to where you are going. Consider it part of your road map. Just like in any journey you have to start out developing a course of action or creating a path.

During my search I observed one big mistake that occurs after someone loses their job and that is their lack of focus and preparation, and this leads to a loss of self esteem as well as confidence. You cannot rely on anything or anyone at this time. Get a plan together and start the ball rolling. The competition out there is fiercer than ever and you cannot afford to drag your feet. Each and every day is important and losing just one day could result in an extra month or two in job search mode. Consider hiring a career coach that will keep you on track. Career coaches are not just temporary but can offer long term advice. They will deal with everything from how your emotions are affected and how to handle that to directing you to a doing self-evaluations. They may provide you with self-assessment tests that will determine your strengths and any weakness. Don't expect this to be a one-time counseling session. You may find that it will be best to be an ongoing method. Fee's for career counselors can either be flat fees or hourly, from $50-$200 per hour. If you decide to take this path, make sure your counselor is certified. As with many professions, there are those out there that practice unscrupulous methods and are more concerned with taking your money.

Setting goals is another step in the plan. You need to have something to reach for or a map of where you are going. Most likely you have spent many hours thinking and dreaming of where you would like to be. It may be something as simple as losing five pounds or it could be that Alaskan cruise. Whatever it is, you have got to put it down on paper and develop a plan to get there. Decide what you want and determine why it is important to you. You may find out once you put some thought into it that it really is not a significant goal or one that is not important. For example, one time I spoke to someone who was into sailing and I decided I wanted to try it someday. Each time I put together my annual goals I included sailing. For whatever reasons, I never made a strong attempt to attempt sailing. Then one day I questioned myself why I was not making a valid attempt at it and realized it was not a real goal after all. It just sounded good at the time and I just kept listing it. When I realized it was not important I just replaced it with a goal more suited to my dreams and desires. Specific goals are not permanent. As you attain certain goals, you can replace them or adjust them. If you feel a goal is not practical, then find another and replace it.

You have to determine what benefits of achieving the goal will surface. If there are no benefits, then perhaps this is not a goal you need to be putting effort into. Perhaps it is not an intelligent goal. For example, if you are six foot six and weigh two hundred fifty pounds and you have a dream of being a jockey then it is time to rethink that goal. But, there may be a compatible goal to replace it with. You may find that purchasing a horse and riding it in the country on weekends will satisfy that yearning. Make sure the goal is yours and not someone else's, because you will not accomplish it if so. Your heart will not be in it. That does not mean that if your spouse has a goal of traveling to Europe and you just as soon go to Hawaii that it should not be important. The wording of your goal should be to assist your spouse in their dream of going to Europe. Make it fun and you both will be happy. If it is important, then take the necessary action to move towards it. As you delve into each goal make sure you uncover any possible barriers that will hinder your pursuit and work out a plan to overcome them. When you sit down with pen in hand listing your goals, make sure they are within your principles and ethics. Accomplishing a goal that you feel guilty about will prove to be a bad experience.

There are four periods of time that you must account for. First, set immediate goals. These are goals for tomorrow, next week, next month, and anything up to one year. The next period of time is one-two year goals, then 2-5 years and finally more than 5 years. Each goal should follow the SMART format:

Specific **M**easurable **A**ttainable **R**ealistic **T**ime Bound

Goals should be specific with no loose ends. Stating you are going to win a race does not provide any specifics. Which race? Why? When? Where? Provide enough details that make the goal clear. Measuring each one of your goals gives you a direction. Stating you are going to lose weight could be best measured by stating you are going to lose 10 pounds in 60 days. If you just state you are going to lose weight, you have no goal or direction. You could lose two pounds in a week and be satisfied that your goal is met. Put it down on paper. Attainability is important because you don't want to set a goal that is impossible. For example, stating you are going to lose 20 pounds in two days is next to ridiculous. You don't want to make the goal too easy. Stating you are going to lose five pounds in the next ten months may be attainable but not challenging. Being realistic follows next and relating it to the weight, stating you are going to lose 10 pounds in 60 days is realistic. The 60 days also makes it time bound. You now have all the ingredients in setting a goal.

Set up a tracking sheet and if you are unfamiliar with setting goals then perhaps it is best to start with daily goals. Don't just set job search goals but incorporate other personal goals as well. Fitness, financial, spiritual and personal achievement goals should also be incorporated. Don't let your life encompass only those goals relating to a job search. You must not only be diversified in your job search methods but also in your personal life to include family. You will find this has an indirect bearing on your job search and career once you become employed. Start daily or weekly and then build from there. You want to have long-range goals as well as short-range goals.

- The following chart is an example of what you can use to begin charting your goals.

CATEGORY	GOAL	SUN	MON	TUE	WED	THU	FRi	SAT
Resumes Sent	5 per week							
Networking Events	5 per week							
Spiritual Time	4 hrs week							
Fitness	5 hrs week							
Family Time	3 hrs week							

You can also build a chart that covers the entire month giving you a picture view of your accomplishments over the last few weeks. This enables you to see the direction you are heading in, whether you are improving your lifestyle or reverting back to old habits. Play with it for several weeks until you find that which works best for you. Goals can be adjusted as you go along. For example, you may realize that your goal was not challenging enough two months down the road and it needs to be increased or perhaps you were overly optimistic with the goal and it has to be reduced. Constantly review your goals, not only to adjust but to keep them in the forefront of your mind.

We will get more into the financial aspect of the job search in a following chapter; however this has to be part of your plan. You need to determine your "panic" date, that date which your plan is no longer sufficient. Perhaps this is the time when your severance or unemployment funds run out. It may be longer such as when your savings runs out. The plan must include a financial evaluation. Review your assets, income and expenditures. What cash do you have on hand or what liquidities are available. The plan must allow for the long haul. There is an unwritten rule that for every $10,000 in salary you desire, it will be one month of job searching. For example, if your desired salary is $50,000, prepare to be out of work five months. Keep in mind this is an estimate and it could take more or less time. Many financial planners will advise you to have six months worth of funds in the bank for situations like this but keep in mind that if your desired salary level is upwards of $70,000 or more, then based on the $10,000 per month guideline, six months savings is not enough.

Finding a job is a job. It cannot be taken lightly nor can you wait for the good fairy to ring your doorbell with an offer. You must be aggressive in your search as well as your planning for the search. The more efficient the plan the less aggravation you will have in your search. You must have faith and look for spiritual guidance. There may have been a reason for your loss of employment. The answers to this may be found in your assessments. Maybe the answer will not come until you find your next career position.

The job market is different than it was ten years ago. Companies are more specialized than they ever were. In the past you may have performed three or four functions that are now performed by several different employees within specific departments. For example, in the financial services field, branch offices of finance companies used to perform their own marketing, mortgage closings and collections, just to name a few. Each of these functions is now done by different departments. Collections within many companies are actually being done in call centers for an entire region or company. Hiring groups and decision makers are no longer the same person or group. Human Resource departments actually are now even broken up with a department for recruiters who just have the sole responsibility of locating qualified potential candidates. Some companies even outsource their background checks. Many times in the past the decision to hire someone was made by the immediate supervisor. That supervisor now is just another cog in the wheel and may not even have the ability to make the final decision. The job market has become much more competitive.

Higher education has become more important. It was not that many years ago that as long as you had a high school diploma you could qualify for a position yet now a Master's degree is required for the same positions. It is estimated that the average person will have more than 10 jobs in their career. Just ten years ago it was not uncommon to see employees retiring from a company with 20, 25 or 30 years employment with the same company. I have a friend who is employed with a large financial services company and has been there 40 years.

If you do not have the necessary degrees, perhaps this is an appropriate time to continue your education. There are many colleges as well as Internet programs available that makes it easier than it used to be. Distant learning has become a billion dollar enterprise and it has enabled many professionals to advance their career whether it is simply taking a refresher course or obtaining undergraduate and graduate degrees. Many major colleges offer distant learning programs. Other colleges have weekend programs that afford you the opportunity to advance your education without affecting work hours or other commitments during the week. Visit your local library to scan books on distant learning or simply go to the web. Look for trade magazines for your profession. They sometimes have classified ad sections.

Let's spend some time on your plan, but before we do that there are some simple organizational steps you should take. First, stay focused on your objective. As we stated previously, locating a job is a job, most probably harder work than you ever performed for your previous employer. Don't procrastinate at any stage. For every day you delay, ten others have moved past you. Next, set up a home office. This will be where you will be spending much of your time. Make sure you have the necessary supplies: pen, paper, etc. Just like you had in your desk at work. Also, a computer and printer are vital to your job search. If you have a fax machine, that adds more to your search but don't purchase one. You can work around this, as there are many stores where you can fax the necessary documents for a small fee. With the recent progress in technology, rarely will you have to fax a resume. Almost all companies provide you the opportunity to email the resume or have websites where you can simply download it.

There should be a telephone in your office as well as a calendar. You cannot perform a solid job search without this equipment. Your office should be in a quiet area of your home where you can close the door and not be disturbed. If you have young children, you need to make sure you are not interrupted.

Have your spouse assist you here by keeping the children occupied. It may be necessary to continue with childcare during the day. It may prove to be cost effective, allowing you sufficient time for your search. You need to be able to take phone calls as they occur and you may leave for an interview at a moment's notice, although this is rare. Make sure you do set time aside to spend with your children, as they will not understand why you are behind closed doors and will want your attention. Whenever you are at home, dress as if you are at work. Don't sit around the computer in your pajamas. Have good posture at your desk.

    A briefcase is another valuable tool. It should be equipped as to where you can grab it on the run. Make sure you have office supplies in it as well as a good supply of your resume. Also, you should have thank you cards and stamps in the briefcase. Included should be an ample supply of business cards. Business cards can be purchased at most office supply stores such as Office Depot and Staples. You can also purchase the stock and print them yourself off your home computer. One other viable source for business cards is at www.vistaprint.com where you can purchase cards free except for the cost of shipping, which is less than ten dollars. But heed this warning, you need a business card. You must act like a professional to be taken for one. Some career counselors feel you should have your occupation listed on the business card. For example, if you are in marketing, state this. If it is a technology field, again state this. As we discuss networking in a future chapter you will see why this is important. I would also suggest you purchase some form of holder for the business cards you receive. You may find it invaluable when you need to refer back to a prior networking source. Most stationary and discount stores carry business card holders or you can purchase a clear view sheet that is made to hold business cards and place in a three ring binder. In everything you do you must treat this job search as a business project.

    Also make a name tag for your jacket or blouse. This will prove beneficial in your networking events. You can purchase kits with five or six plastic name tag holders as well as the stock to make the actual card. Maybe you can share the cost with another one of your job search friends. Next time you are at a local job fair, look to see how few actually have a name tag on yet, it will be noticed by the companies that you speak with at the job fair. Many will take note of it and that may very well carry over into a possible interview. They will immediately set you apart from the rest and see your professionalism.

You may want to set up a three ring binder to track all of your efforts. You could have all of the business cards you obtained in the front, followed by a tracking sheet of your efforts. It is suggested you sit down and set goals of contacts you wish to make in the upcoming week. Some areas you would need to include would be:

Networking events
Job fairs to attend
Informational interviews
Contacts: those who know decision makers
Contacts with peers, friends, relatives
Contacts with networking partners
Phone contacts with decision makers
Phone contacts with peers
Written communication with decision makers
Written communication with all contacts
Internet search time
Number of positions applied for
Total time spent on job search

If you are to receive unemployment compensation you will need to track your efforts; those companies that you applied to whether in person or via phone. This three ring binder is an excellent place to keep the tracking form. The unemployment office will most likely supply you with the first blank form and you can make copies for the future. In addition, each job you apply for through the Internet will have a job description. Print a copy of this for your book. This will serve two purposes: to have a record for the unemployment office as well as all the details of the position should you get an interview. Another way, if you do not wish to print them is create a folder in your Outlook file and save them there. You may even want to create a journal for any contacts you make. This would include target companies or potential positions and the contact person for each, to include phone numbers and email addresses, as well as the date and results of your last contact. This job description can provide key words for the resume you will submit for the position. You will find that you will refer back to this at times. Be as detailed as possible as your memory could fail you at a later, but important time. Should you have a phone interview, you can have this in front of you, keeping you informed to key words in the job description. It may even impress the interviewer that you know so much about the company.

What many individuals have found helpful is having an accountability partner. This is someone who is searching for a new position as you are. Meet with them weekly, either by phone or for coffee. Review your previous results when you meet. This helps to keep you honest and dedicated to your search. Just make sure your partner is just as aggressive as you and does not bring you down. This is not the same as your mentor or a member of your management team. This person shares a similar goal in that they are unemployed as well. They may be able to offer suggestions to you or perhaps even know hiring individuals at your target company. They do not have to be in the same profession as you. Everyone's job search should be based on identical search tools.

One tool that many unemployed people are not aware of or do not make any effort at is having a marketing plan. This serves you in cases where it is not appropriate to have a resume. It may be when you are having coffee with a potential employer or just a person who knows a lot of decision makers. This marketing plan also serves as a tool to keep you focused on where you are going. It does not replace a resume nor should it ever be submitted to apply for a position. This plan just gives those who read it a roadmap to where you want to go. Targeting certain vital areas gives a strong indication of your route.

This marketing plan would have the following:

- Heading would be set up just like your resume, with all appropriate contact info
- Executive Summary section detailing your professional objective, positioning statement that shows your background in two sentences and a third paragraph that lists your expertise
- Section titled Target Positioning that will give your target position, preferred geographical preference, target industries, and target companies

On the following pages are sample marketing plans but the format can be altered to fit your needs and desires. Do not feel it has to be a carbon copy of the sample plan. Be creative but keep it professional. The plan should not be burdensome. It should reflect where you want to go and how you want to get there. It is not a resume and should not be presented as one to a recruiter.

Sample Marketing Plan:

John Doe

123 Elm St. Home: 555-123-4567
Any town, USA 12345 Cell: 404-234-5668

jdoe@aol.com

Executive Summary

Professional Objective: To secure a position in marketing for a Fortune 500 company.

Positioning Statement: Results oriented professional with over 20 years in consumer product sales. Proven success in marketing to large corporations.

Expertise: Marketing experience in consumer, telecom and computer products.

Target Function: Marketing VP or Marketing Director

Target Geographics: Boston, Massachusetts

Target Industries: Consumer products

Target Companies: XYZ Corporation, ABC Marketing, Boston Telecom

PAUL RYAN

MARKETING PLAN

1122 Hampton Lane Orlando, FL. 32809	Home: 407-651-5689 Cell: 407.456-6547

EXECUTIVE SUMMARY

Professional Objective: To secure a position in a credit union or call center utilizing my background in lending, collections, and customer service to develop a team second to none.

Professional Summary: Results oriented professional with over 20 years experience in financial services. Proven success in developing outstanding customer service foundations through strong team development programs.

Expertise:

Strategic Planning: Formulated plans for new branch operations

P&L responsibility for multi-unit branches and call center operations.

Lending: Knowledgeable in automobile, commercial, mortgage and retail lending

Collections: Experienced in automobile, commercial, credit card, and mortgage portfolios

Call Center: Led teams in inbound & outbound call centers.

Customer Service: Recognized for "outrageous customer service

TARGETING

Target Functions: Vice President or Director **Target Industries:** Lending, Collections, Customer Service and Financial Services
Organizational Culture: Mid-large growth oriented company

ACCOMPLISHMENTS

- Lending > Top District Manager in loan volume
- Collections > Reduced delinquency by over 5% in three different operations.
- Operations > Opened up new multi branch operation & achieved profit 6 mo. ahead of schedule.
- Staffing > Reduced employee turnover by 25% and developed new hiring procedures.

GEOGRAPHICAL PREFERENCE

Orlando   Lakeland   Tampa

TARGET COMPANIES

Credit Unions Call Centers Grow Financial Citigroup Fairwinds Credit Union HSBC

CAREER HISTORY

Avco Financial Services Transamerica Financial Household Finance SouthTrust Bank

COMMUNITY INVOLVEMENT

Church Strategic Planning Church Men's Club

Some of the sources that are available for your job search are listed below. There have been numerous surveys done that state networking produces approximately 75% of the available positions as well as some not even advertised. But this does not necessarily prove your next position will come from networking. You can put 75% of your efforts here but it is suggested you become as diversified as possible to secure that next position. To put it mildly, put your hands in each of the pots. The gold could be at the bottom of any one of them. Recently I met with a recruiter at a large company for an informational interview and he stated that he rarely hires from job advertisements or Internet postings. Most of his hires come about from networking.

Networking: Friends, relatives, financial planner, attorney, physician, banker, or your next-door neighbor. You never know whose brother or sister is the decision maker at one of your target companies. Attendance at meetings and volunteer events is crucial. You must be highly visible. Create a high profile around your community.

Newspaper Ads: Your local newspaper is another source although not as good as it once was prior to the Internet days. Most newspapers have one day that is more effective than others. This will be the day when most companies advertise their open positions, and usually this is the Sunday edition. Don't forget to review the business section of the newspaper to see what is going on in your community.

Internet: Monster.com and Careerbuilder.com are only two of the many available.

Employment agencies: Your local unemployment office.

Recruiters: More commonly known as headhunters.

Business pages: Many newspapers have special inserts once a week that deals with the business world.

Trade Organizations/Unions: Many professions have some form of union or trade organization that may even meet weekly or monthly. These same organizations may have trade magazines or publications.

Government agencies, usually local, may have job search tools for you to pursue.

Yellow pages of phone book: Look through the pages to locate companies that may need your services.

Chamber of Commerce: Most cities have chambers that may be able to offer you some assistance such as lists of companies in your chosen field.

Library: Research your desired industry in the reference area of the library.

These are but a few of the resources to assist you in your job search. A note of caution here is that once you have a live prospect, whether you have interviewed or not, don't back off of your job search. As confident as you might be on obtaining the job, it is not definite. Don't lose out on any opportunities because you were confident you had a job "in the bag". That bag has a way of having holes in it. This is not meant to discourage you when you have just completed a solid interview. It is meant to convince you to stay focused and as the old saying goes "Do not put all of your eggs in one basket." Stay motivated in your search. Listen to motivational CD's and tapes that can be obtained through your local library. Listen to them as you travel to your networking events. You will find there are so many great motivational speakers out there. To name a few, Denis Waitley, Stephen Covey, Napoleon Hill, Tony Robbins and my personal favorite, Zig Ziglar. All have written several good books as well as recorded excellent motivational CD's or DVD's. Once you locate that dream position purchase some of these CD's or DVD's to continue listening at your convenience. They will certainly always help you in staying motivated on your new job and perhaps help you advance in that position as well. Many of these speakers tour the country speaking at large gatherings. You may be able to get your employer to pay for you attending these speaking engagements because you can bring this material back to your team to help motivate them.

One other area I would like to touch on is your scheduling. Just getting up in the morning and deciding what you want to do that particular day in your job search is not fruitful. You have to create a schedule for at least one week out and more preferably two weeks out. During my job search I always maintained 30 days of calendaring. Eliminate as much white space as possible.

This means that you do not want to have a day where you see nothing listed. This includes the weekend but here you are scheduling your family and leisure time. There will be times when you just need to rejuvenate yourself and a day to yourself is just what the doctor ordered. Sit down and do some crossword puzzles or start a jigsaw puzzle. Take in one of your local free attractions such as an art or history museum. This is just as important as the networking events you have listed. Remember that your family needs your support as much as you need theirs so schedule time with them, even if it is just playing in the back yard or a ride to the beach. They will appreciate what you are going through more and will more likely allow you private, uninterrupted work time.

Some of the items you would list on your schedule are:

    Family time
    Career counselor meetings
    Internet Health
    Networking meetings
    Financial Meetings with centers of influence such as coffee time
    Interviews
    Telephone contacts
    Volunteering
    Organizational time
    Spiritual time

There are many other items you could list. Do not get too restrictive on your scheduling, as there are things that arise. If you have a slot scheduled for organizational time and a recruiter wants to schedule an interview, reschedule the organizational time. You must be somewhat flexible as you create this calendar. Always keep this schedule in your briefcase and with you at all times so that if you are having coffee with a networking source and you receive a phone call from a recruiter you can be accurate in the scheduling. This also provides a good tool to sit down with your management team and let them know what you are doing. Not only will they better understand how your time is spent, but also they may have some good suggestions. If you have Outlook software on your computer, take full advantage of it. Use the calendar for scheduling interviews or job fairs. You can also create folders for documents. You may want a folder for your networking leads or for keeping follow up emails from reliable sources. Keep any emails that relate to your job search. If you delete one and it turns out that the person who sent it to you had included information about a potential job source that does not interest you today but may tomorrow, creates a lost opportunity.

One last comment is that abide by the 80/20 rule in that 80% of your results should be coming from 20% of your efforts and not the reverse. If you are wheel spinning then it will be that much longer until you find that next position. And the longer you are wheel spinning your savings will be drained even further. Remember, keep your faith up and direct yourself to this new, exciting challenge.

Let's talk a little about email communication as this will be a common method of communication during your job search. In fact, much of this can also be used in your professional career once you land. When you send out an email make sure there is some explanation of the email in the subject line. It should not be any longer than six words and is used to introduce the reader to the topic you will be addressing. Never use all caps as this insinuates you are yelling online. Begin with a name and greeting and perhaps some small talk but keep it professional. Do not use "I" as the first word in the email. This gives the impression that the email is focusing on you. Keep in mind that many emails you send will be kept by the receiver and referred to at a later time. Once you have stated what you want to say, you may need to discuss this further. Finish off the email with something like this: "As your schedule is extremely full, if I do not hear from you by date, I will follow up with you." And do not forget to end it with thank you. One further comment on emails: have your name, email address and phone number set up in your Outlook so that when you send a message, all of the contact information is right there, especially if they need to print it out.

As I stated previously, it is also suggested that you have some downtime or personal time. This should be a time when you can go off and be by yourself and reflect on your status. It does not just have to be about the job search, it can be about other things in your personal life. Perhaps when you were employed there were many things you failed to do. Did you spend sufficient time with your family or attend church regularly? Reflect on the direction your life has led you. But I caution you, this is not just about negativity…you must see the good things your life has produced. Think about the times that bring smiles to your face. It may be something such as the home run your son hit in his Little League game or that your daughter made captain of her cheerleading squad. You are faced with enough negativity in your job search. Now is the time to see all the good things you have accomplished. This quiet time should be spent with no interruptions such as a long walk on the beach, take a hike through the woods or maybe just a drive out in the country. Alternate your time with your significant other but again, do not make this about the job search. Both of you need some laughs and smiles during this trying time.

One final comment before we move on is that do not procrastinate in your search. The speed of sound is 768 mph (at 68 degrees and sea level). At 767 you have not reached the speed of sound. The point I want to make here is that one extra degree makes all of the difference in the world. The same is true of your job search, get that extra degree in your job search efforts. During my business development days I used a method that proved quite advantageous for me. I would schedule myself to do 10 business development calls per day. When I finished that 10th call I would make one extra call. This annualized out to an extra 260 calls per year. If my normal success rate on those 10 calls was just 20%, then annually I would add 52 more clients/customers to my portfolio. Just a little extra effort creates large numbers.

"A man can be as great as he wants to be. If you believe in yourself and have the courage, the determination, the dedication, the competitive drive and if you are willing to sacrifice the little things in life and pay the price for the things that are worthwhile, it can be done."

-Vince Lombardi

DON'T QUIT

Joe David Harrison

When things go wrong as they sometimes will,
When the road you're trudging seems all uphill,
When the funds are low and the debts are high,
And you want to smile but you have to sign,
When care is pressing you down a bit,
Rest, if you must, but don't you quit.
Life is queer with its twists and turns,
As every one of us sometimes learns,
And many a failure turns about
When he might have won had he stuck it out;
Don't give up though the pace seems slow—
You may succeed with another blow.
Success is failure turned inside out—
The silver tint of the clouds of doubt,
And you never can tell how close you are,
It may be near when it seems so far;
So stick to the fight when you're hardest hit
It's when things seem worst that you must not quit!

2.
MISSION AND VISION STATEMENTS

THE NEXT STEP IN YOUR PLAN IS TO DEVELOP MISSION AND VISION Statements. Both serve as clarification of the direction you want to take. They also serve as a road map and both go deep inside of you and bring out what you are made of. Neither will indicate that you really like Rap music rather than the Country Western you currently listen to. They won't state that you really like the 49ers when you live in Boston. They won't even indicate that you like one kind of peanut butter over another. What they will do is help you understand what is important to you. You may have gotten away from some of your values that have been a big part of your life. Sometimes we work for employers who unknowingly help us in hiding these values. There have been many cases where potential financial gains have super-ceded what someone truly believed in. Also, there may be pressure from employers to produce, but in ways that cloud our good judgment. Now is the time to uncover these values and correct where needed. Some state that it could take up to six months and perhaps longer to create Mission and Vision Statements. You certainly don't have that long if you are out of work. But keep in mind that these statements are the result of intensive thought and effort. Your original Mission and Vision Statements will change, over and over again. This does not indicate you did not put sufficient thought into it the first time but, that as you grow so does your direction. It is something like that first home you bought. When the builder was constructing it, the front yard was all dirt. When they finished it they put sod down and it looked better. A month later it looked even better because now you could not see where a piece of sod stopped and the next one began and it was greener. The grass all blended together. As you mow and fertilize the sod it now becomes a lawn. Each year, assuming you continue to take care of it, the lawn improves. There is no difference in your Mission and Vision Statements. As you continually "fertilize" them they become better and better.

It does not matter whether you complete the Mission or Vision Statement first. Some think it is better to complete the Vision Statement first while others chose the Mission. I feel the Mission Statement should be completed first because the Vision Statement is actually the result of what your Mission Statement is. What you must do is start working on both. Go off to a quiet spot and think about what you really want out of your professional life. Find a quiet spot on the beach, hibernate in your den or just sit in the far corner of your backyard in a comfortable chair. Locate a spot where you can think, uninterrupted. Bring paper and pencil and start jotting down the ideas. The first thought might be regarding the Mission Statement, yet the next thought might fall under the Vision. Sort them out later. Get the juices flowing. This chapter will first look at the Mission Statement and second the Vision. Both the Mission and Vision Statements are not written like your college essay. They need only be two or three lines. This is one reason why you need to put so much thought into creating them. In these three lines you have to condense much of what comes out of your thoughts. Writing five or six paragraphs does not summarize everything. If you need to write that much, create a Life Plan and make that the introduction. Perhaps you may have to do that first to get all of your thoughts on paper. After that is completed go back over it and use a hi-liter to bring out the top items.

When writing the Mission and Vision Statements, do not be wordy. You are not looking to write a book. This is not meant to impress someone else. Your statements should be self-inspiring and motivational. Both can cover your personal as well as your professional life. In fact, I would suggest it because, should you have separate values? Of course not. This is what is in your soul, what you believe in and the direction you want to go. Perhaps you started out right as an adult both in your personal and professional life but fell off course. This is the opportunity to get back on track and perhaps build on those original values. Both the Mission and Vision Statements should be clear and concise. You do not want to sit down six months from now and wonder what they meant. In addition, there may come a time that you share these with your spouse, mentor or career search partner and it should be clear to them who you are. When you first complete each one I would suggest you read it each day, just before you go off on your search to remind yourself of who you are. Once you locate your career position it is still necessary to review them both from time to time. Again, this will keep you on track. Of course, always look for opportunities to fine tune them. Remember, both have to be what you truly believe in. They must address what you value in life. Be realistic in their completion. Don't go shooting for the stars; however a little aggressive dreaming is warranted.

The Mission Statement should indicate what your priority in life is. What is the direction you want to go in? What are you really devoted to in life? Keep in mind that although God and family are top priorities you want to gear this toward your professional life. Yet God and family do play a role here. They are the foundation of your professional life. You may have to sit with your significant other to help unlock some thoughts. Ask them to be brutally honest with you. Maybe some of your values have become tainted over the years and this is a good opportunity to find out which are out of line.

Once the Mission Statement is complete you want to ensure it is meaningful, not just some words on paper. Anyone can do that for you. One idea is to have your spouse or significant other write what they think your direction is. That may truly enlighten you. It may also uncover some bad habits or misdirection on your part and you never even realized it. Both the Mission and Vision Statements will assist you in directing your efforts as well as energy in the right direction. Keep in mind that right now you want to focus only on your present direction, that being where you want to go now. Your present direction is not the same as it was yesterday. All of your efforts now are aimed at improving your professional life along with your personal life. You will find they will overlap each other. This effort may indicate that you put too much work in some areas and not enough work in other areas. Do not be afraid to be critical of yourself. The purpose of this effort is to create or improve that new direction.

Undoubtedly, you will have to adjust the Mission Statement as you go, but this is just fine-tuning. You should not have to completely rewrite it, yet even that might be advisable down the road. Initially you want to create some direction and get the car in gear. With progress comes change. As you follow your Mission Statement you may realize that there are other deep feelings within you that were previously suppressed. I met a man once that was in the mortgage lending business for many years. He had lost his position one day and decided he wanted to become involved in training others how to sell. He was good at it and excelled at educating others how to sell mortgages. He loved his job but one day he realized that what he loved was teaching but he loved his faith more and that actually led him into teaching at a Christian school. Although his income was reduced dramatically, his values became primary and money became secondary. Obviously his original Mission Statement needed some revision.

The Mission Statement actually defines your objectives. In the above case the original statement unknowingly did not do that. However, when he originally completed the Mission Statement he felt it had defined his objective. He had indicated that once he created his very first Statement he had to adjust his selling techniques because they were not of the sound principles he had inside of him. Perhaps his Mission Statement, and yours, may be a series of steps in bringing out all of your values. His original Statement helped him to create selling techniques that were of a higher integrity yet in the long run these same steps directed him towards a greater calling.

What you have to do is determine what your objective is. What is your passion in life? Is there something you want to deliver in your professional life? The gentleman above ultimately wanted to deliver education within the Christian faith. Stephen Covey also states that creating the Mission Statement is more about "the process than the results". The process is when you are in the creative stages, such as when you are out there sitting on the beach jotting down the ideas. You will find that you can spend eight hours there jotting down these thoughts yet two days later you will change your direction or new ideas will emerge. When I created my Statement, I rewrote it over and over 20 times. Just two years later I created an entirely new Statement. Your final creation will ultimately indicate what you really want out of life. You may think you know now what you want but so did our Christian educator above.

You will find that when you create the Mission Statement it will help you strategize how you will pursue your new position. It, as mentioned earlier, will provide a road map to your direction. You may have been in the financial services field for the last twenty years but you realized your passion was actually teaching others and perhaps that may direct you to a life of education or a position in your Christian faith. There are many cases where someone in their forty's has changed careers in mid field and became a school teacher, giving up very lucrative careers.

The development of the Mission Statement has to be your work. You can't pay someone to create it for you such as in the case of a resume. You may have to have your spouse help you put it into words but the thoughts have to come directly from you and those soul-seeking moments you spent on the beach or in the back yard. There are sources that you can use to get you started. With technology, everything is right at your fingertips and only seconds away. Earl Nightingale has a website that assists you in creating a Mission Statement for free. Simply go to www.nightingale.com/mission to get started now. There are many other sources on the web as well. As stated previously you will have to continually review and make any necessary changes to the Mission Statement. Obviously, you don't want to spend all this time creating a Statement and stick it in a drawer. Set a goal to read it once a week. This will keep you focused and keep you from going astray in your direction, just as you do when you are using a road map.

Here are several examples of Mission Statements. They will provide you with some indication of where to start.

"My mission is to dedicate myself to fulfilling a passion of educating others on the proper use of personal credit. Continuing to show each of my peers and students the correct way to build financial wealth without thoughts of personal gain fuel my desire to see a more financial secure family exist."

"It is my desire to use my knowledge and past experiences to teach the members of my church God's way for sound marriages.

I will put all of my focus into showing each couple the correct way to build a long lasting marriage and family."

"I have a passion for building solid teams that encourage great morale and outstanding customer service. This passion will further be used to train each employee to be the best they can be."

Following is the Mission Statement for Toastmasters clubs:

"The mission of a Toastmasters club is to provide a mutually supportive and positive learning environment in which every member has the opportunity to develop communication and leadership skills, which in turn foster self-confidence and personal growth."

The Mission Statement of Nightingale-Conant is as follows:

"To be the preeminent publisher and provider of self-improvement resources that inspires and empowers individuals to lead the lives they most desire".

General Motors:

"Our mission is to acknowledge the problems facing General Motors, develop turnaround plans, build for profit, reposition for growth, and strengthen the GM organization."

Let's cover some Vision Statements now that we have a firm understanding of Mission Statements. Vision Statements cover your values. What are your values? Did any arise during your thought process creating the Mission? Do you fully understand what your values are? Are your values now what they were ten years ago? Have you strayed away from what your true values are? This is a great time to answer all of these questions. Again, here we only want two or three lines, basically a paragraph. It need not be wordy or flamboyant. As with the Mission Statement you want to focus on your direction and not the past. The Vision Statement must be clear, concise and not overly dramatic.

Although it will most likely be for your eyes only, keep it professional. This is just a further indication of the efforts needed to make it meaningful.

Your passions should show here as well. The Vision Statement is similar to the Mission Statement although it should provide a clearer picture. You know what your mission is so now is a good time to indicate how you are going to fulfill it. Just as its name, this is your vision on accomplishing your mission. The how and how to of it all, so to speak. Now you may think this is your professional view, but keep in mind it is your personal view as well. It is what you are all about inside. Here is also a case where you want to refer back to your spouse or even your entire management team. They may have some ideas, after knowing your mission, which will provide further direction for you. But, it cannot be entirely their thoughts. This is YOUR vision, not theirs. Draw primarily from what is inside of you. These thoughts are the core of your being. Don't get away from what you really see. As in the Mission Statement you will have to continually review and adjust this as well.

Here are some examples of Vision Statements:

General Motors:

"GM's vision is to be the world leader in transportation products and related services. We will earn our customers' enthusiasm through continuous improvement driven by the integrity, teamwork, and innovation of GM people."

Baskin Robbins Ice Cream:

"World's Greatest Cookie and Treat Store"

Sprint:

"To be a world-class telecommunications company—the standard by which others are measured."

After reading each of the previous vision statements you can now see that this is the how-to of the plan. You developed the Mission Statement indicating where you want to go and now the Vision Statement will show you the plan to accomplish the mission. There is no right or wrong way. Only you can determine if it works for you. Do not worry about perfecting it at this time; just get one down on paper. Remember, you will be adjusting it from time to time. Once the Mission and Vision Statements are complete, you can go out into the world and find that career position that will truly satisfy you. The last few words of the Toastmasters International Vision Statement say it all: "find the courage to change."

"There is more to us than we know. If we can be made to see it, perhaps for the rest of our lives we will be unwilling to settle for less."

-Kurt Hahn

3.
SPIRITUAL

"Let all bitterness, and wrath, and anger, and clamour, and evil speaking, be put away from you, with all malice"
-Ephesians 4:31

DON'T FEEL GUILTY BECAUSE YOU LEFT YOUR LAST JOB WITH anger or anxiety. Many have felt the same way but you must get over it. First, as stated above, it should not be part of your character. God has made it clear that all bitterness should depart from oneself. Think those thoughts only for a minute because it is natural, and then move on with your life. Continuing to hold these thoughts disappoints our Lord. He expects better from us. If you drag these thoughts with you, it will only fester and cause you spiritual as well as mental and physical harm. In addition, it will carry over into your job search. What will that first interviewer think when you spout off some of those feelings? They may even come out without you realizing it. You do not want to lose another position, perhaps even better than the last because of some unnecessary feelings. I recently spoke to a human resources director of a large consumer products company who looks for these red flags at interviews. He looks at answers to the interview questions as well as their body language. If the candidate is presented with a sensitive question and they answer confidently with little body language, he stands out from the rest of the candidates. If they suddenly hunch their shoulders, then there is some concern and further discussion on that particular question will be necessary. It could just prove to be nervousness but that will come out in further conversation.

If you have been a strong Christian and your faith does not waiver, then you will be better off than most. Should your faith be strong, then you will be able to better cope with the entire situation and realize that God will provide you with direction and wisdom. Don't let these new, unpleasant circumstances rock your faith. These are times when even more emphasis has to be placed on your faith. Spend time daily reading the Bible and set aside personal prayer time. This time should be when there will be few interruptions from family members. Spending this time with the Lord will help you to weather all that will be thrown at you. During trying times we tend to forget the good things that life has brought us. We should not do this. If we focus on only the negativity we see in our daily life, then our life will be exactly that….negativity. In your prayer, give thanks for the good tidings you have received. If you stop and think, there are countless blessings that you have received.

God wants us to live a spiritual life. This can be accomplished by believing in Him. In Mark 11:24 it is stated "Therefore I say unto you, what things soever ye desire, when ye pray, believe that ye receive them, and ye shall have them." Put those evil thoughts aside and direct your mind to believing that God will make everything better and provide you with an even better life. Maybe that last position was not what you really wanted. Maybe the next one and the one following will be better. Yes, I said the one following. The next position you receive may not be your last if the Bureau of Labor Statistics Longitudal Survey is correct. This survey states that the average number of jobs in the age bracket of 18 to 40 in the years 1978 thru 2004 were as follows:

Men: 10.70
Women: 10.30

Pretty scary, isn't it? You are probably sitting there right now, as I did several times, thinking how hard you worked at that last position, how you progressed up the corporate ladder, and how you achieved all the goals that were put before you. I remember having one position where I opened the doors daily at 7:30 am and left most nights no earlier than 6:30 pm and quite often later, as well as worked every other Saturday, at the same time achieving the best results the company ever realized, only to lose the position. And of course, I ate lunch at my desk. Perhaps the end result was God's way of slowing me down. Life is too short and it took the loss of this position for me to see that. We may not like it but it certainly makes sense. Think about your own situation and is it similar to my situation described above?

Each time you lose a position your confidence takes a beating. Self esteem drops. Your mind becomes wrought with negative thoughts. You may even show this attitude in front of your family, those who are there to support you. Is it fair to them to be treated like they were the one who were responsible for your termination? What you have to do is find that lost confidence and build upon it, and that must begin with having faith in God. In Mark 11:22 the Bible states "And Jesus answering saith unto them, Have faith in God." Simple and to the point.

God wants us to be confident. He knows that it is necessary to keep the confidence strong in order to work our way through our daily trials and tribulations. Your confidence will be rocked, especially that first day of unemployment. You will sit there wondering where to go from here, how are you going to pay the mortgage, or how will you be able to take care of your family. You are not the only one that has gone through this. And I simply say to you, get over it! Move on and find ways to answer those questions you have. Having yourself a pit party will not find you a job any faster, so get over it and move on. Believe that everything will improve for the better. God has a plan and you are a key figure in it. Lying in bed stressing over the lack of results from your job search only develops poor health. There will be days when recruiters and human resource professionals won't return your calls or that you were not chosen for the position you felt you were perfect for. Get over it and look for ways to improve your job search.

"It is better to trust in the Lord than to put confidence in man."
-Psalms 118:8

Maybe your first day out of work should be spent visiting your Pastor. Explain to him what happened and what you are going through. Your church may even be able to offer you financial assistance until you get back on your feet. The Pastor will not reject you nor will your church abandon you because

God is there watching over you. Keep in mind that your Pastor knows many people and he may provide some job search assistance. Now maybe you have not been attending church, so what better time to meet your new Pastor and see what spiritual blessings your church can offer. Some religions have daily mass or services. Most likely these services begin before you can even accomplish much in your job search. Make it a point to attend daily or as often as you can. If you have not been attending church, then perhaps this is an appropriate time for the entire family to start in a new spiritual direction.

This time out of work provides us with an excellent opportunity to get to know God much better. Allow time to sit by yourself and pray and speak to God. There are books out there that talk about prayer but you will find that they all say to just talk to God like you would a good friend. There is no template on how to pray. God wants to know what is in your heart and how He can help to make things better. You will also find true peace during this time and don't you feel you need some peace and calm at this time? If you don't have one, purchase a Bible. They are inexpensive and can be found at any department store and certainly well worth the expense. Make reading the Bible a daily habit, even after you locate a new position. These times of reflection will provide you with some inner peace and perhaps even clear the cobwebs out. New job search ideas will spring from this reflection. It will also tell you whether or not you have been living your life as you should be. Have you expressed your love to God? If you have been away from church or prayer, then the answer is obvious.

God wants to provide assistance. He wants you to go to Him and ask for help. You may think He was not there before, especially if you were not attending church but He was there watching over you waiting for you to ask for His guidance. He has not forsaken you or become mad because you have not allowed Him into your life. He did not bring this new unfavorable situation into your life, but He is there to assist in making it go away. You will find that as you evolve into a better Christian your life will improve and new problems will still arise but your new attitude will find ways to overcome these problems and any obstacles that arise. It does not matter whether you are Baptist, Catholic, Presbyterian or any other religion, just attend church. There is certainly one close to your home and they will welcome you with open arms….I guarantee it.

"Faith is believing what we do not see. The reward of this faith is to see what we believe."
-St. Augustine

4.
FINANCIAL

WE NOW GET INTO THE FINANCIAL ASPECT OF BEING UNEMPLOYED. THIS is usually the source of much of the panic you will encounter during your search. A word of caution in that you must stay focused. Do not panic. This will only hinder your progress and cause you to make decisions that you may regret later. When you sit down to perform your financial evaluation, one of the first things to come up with is a decision date where you must sit down and adjust your career search with regards to income. This is the date when you feel your back is against the wall; when all the funds are about to be exhausted. I have heard this called the drop dead date, the panic date, and the bankruptcy date. These are words that signify too much negativity. Although the decision date is serious, you cannot over react. The decision date will be when funds are getting extremely low and your current plan of attack must be changed. Perhaps this is the date when you must significantly reduce your salary expectations. It may be the time when you will have to list your home on the market. It may be the date when you have to move back home with family. This date can only be determined by you and only after serious consideration and careful planning.

Before you establish any kind of budget, it is necessary for you to file for unemployment compensation. Do not assume you are not eligible. That determination will be made by your state unemployment office. This can usually be done by phone and the Internet as well as visiting the local office. You will not get in trouble filing even if you do eventually get denied. Once you are approved you most likely can claim your weeks over the Internet or automated telephone system. Make sure you give all the facts that led to your termination. Once you file your claim the unemployment office will contact your previous employer to verify all the details. After a determination is made whether you can receive unemployment compensation or not, and assuming you are approved, you will be promptly notified of the amount of the weekly benefit.

Some of the reasons you may be denied benefits can be that you quit without good cause or were terminated for misconduct relating to your job. It is possible to receive benefits if you quit for good cause, so that is why you must let them make the determination. Once you receive your benefit amount keep in mind taxes will be withheld. At the end of the year you will receive a 1099-G to file with your federal taxes. Normally you will receive a check every other week following your required filing date for claiming weeks. Make sure you stick to the required date and the time to alleviate any chance of losing funds. You will need to keep a record of the attempts you make to locate all suitable employment. When you receive your determination of benefits, a copy of this record form should be attached. There is a possibility you will have to provide this at a later time, so be accurate with the information listed, such as where you applied to, address and contact information, as well as how you applied for the position…online versus personal visit, etc.

Once you sit down with your significant other and determine what your financial status is, you both now must begin putting a plan together. But where are you currently at? What are your assets? What funds do you have available, immediately and long term? What financial obligations do you have? Can any financial obligations be deferred? These are all questions necessary to take stock of what your assets are. You need a financial strategy just like it were a business. Once it is completed you don't just stick it in your desk drawer; you need to review it periodically. Keep it with your financial documents, such as bills, bank accounts, etc.
Your plan must take into account the following:

<u>Assets</u>: Savings accounts, IRA's, Certificate of Deposits, Money Market accounts, stocks and bonds, pensions and real estate.

<u>Misc</u>: Home equity loans available, Visa and Master Card and cash availability.

Liabilities: Rent/mortgage payments, charge card balances, student loans, auto loans; utility expenses such as gas, electric, water, cable, telephone, both home and cell phones.; alimony, child support, tuition, church, health and auto insurance; Heating oils (for cold weather areas), transportation costs; child care.

This information can be obtained by reviewing the last six months amounts for each and every one of your household expenditures. Review your cancelled checks as well as your filing system. You may realize there are some expenses that are out of the ordinary, such as seasonal expenses. This is a great opportunity to review your expenditures and look for ways to reduce some of them. Remember, income is drastically reduced and wherever you can make some positive adjustments will only help in the long run.

Some areas where you can save on expenses are listed below:

- Cutting out grocery coupons from your newspaper or phonebook
- Eliminating snacks
- Dining out, movie rentals, entertainment need to be reduced or eliminated
- Magazine subscriptions
- Create shopping lists before you leave home. Also shop when you are not hungry. Shopping when you are hungry causes unnecessary food expenditures.
- Child care…can you reduce the costs by watching the child yourself or have a member of your family help out during this unemployment period?
- Alcohol and tobacco products
- Reducing electricity expenses by reducing unnecessary use of lighting fixtures
- Dry cleaning
- Lawn or pool care
- Lottery tickets or gambling

There are most likely other areas where you can reduce your expenses. This will be obvious once you review all of your past expenditures. That is why it is practical to review six months worth. That will usually cover all seasonal items as well. On the following page is a sample budget form that you can use to set up your own budget. There are some additional blank lines to allow for your particular case.

LIABILITY	AMOUNT DUE	DATE
MORTGAGE/RENT		
HELOC/2ND MTG PMT		
HOME MAINTENANCE		
TELEPHONE		
ELECTRIC		
GAS/HEATING OIL		
WATER		
CABLE		
NEWSPAPER		
CELL PHONES		
CHURCH		
CHILD CARE		
AUTO INSURANCE		
MEDICAL INSURANCE		
LIFE INSURANCE		
MEDICAL CO-PAYS		
PRESCRIPTIONS		
CHILD SUPPORT		
ALIMONY		
STUDENT LOANS		
MASTERCARD		
VISA		
DEPT STORES		
DEPT STORES		
DEPT STORES		
AUTO LOAN		
AUTO LOAN		
TRANSPORTATION		

Another area to look into is government assistance. There are several programs that you may qualify for. It is appropriate to visit your state Department of Children and Families for assistance. Some areas that you may qualify are:

- Welfare
- Food stamps
- Cash assistance
- Mortgage/rent assistance
- Medicaid

Don't assume you are not entitled to any of them. Again, make the call and take advantage of those available to you. Put your pride aside and use this opportunity to take care of your family. The state government expects you to use these benefits so don't let them down. Remember, the longer you are out of work the more your available assets will become depleted.

Speaking of benefits, let's go back and look at COBRA again. The Consolidated Omnibus Budget Reconciliation Act was enacted in 1986 to give you the ability to continue your group health coverage benefits for a specified period of time, usually 18 months. That's the good news. The bad news is that you are required to pay the entire cost of the premiums. When you were employed you most likely received the benefit of your company paying a portion of the premiums. They are not required to do so once you leave their employ. Of course, you must have been enrolled in the plan at the time of termination. You are not able to start COBRA if you were not in a plan on the date of termination. Assuming you were enrolled, your health benefits will be exactly the same as when you were employed. There is no waiting period or loss of benefits. You will have 60 days to make your decision of whether you want COBRA or not but will be required to pay all premiums due if you desire to continue your insurance. After termination you will receive a notification regarding enrollment in COBRA. This plan may not be the most practical or least expensive available to you so check other sources and see if you can find something more appropriate. If not, then this is one area you will not have to worry about.

Further assistance regarding COBRA can be obtained at the following:

www.dol.gov/ebsa or 1.866.444.3272

U.S. Department of Labor
Employee Benefits Security Administration
Division of Technical Assistance and Inquiries
200 Constitution Avenue NW, Suite N-5619
Washington, DC 20210

Let's discuss income possibilities while you are out of work. Keep in mind that if you are receiving unemployment compensation you must report any income you receive and the appropriate amount will be deducted from your compensation. Look into the possibility of doing consultant work. Does your occupation afford you the knowledge and experience to farm yourself out for consulting work? Many companies use consultants daily and this could give you the opportunity to showcase your talents. Perhaps once you have solved their immediate needs there will be a place on their staff permanently, or consultant work could be your forte. You may find you like this type of work, hours, freedom and even the income.

Contact local temporary employment agencies and look into doing temp work until you land your new position. If you let the agency know up front, you can usually set some flexible hours where you may leave one or two days open for interviews or networking. Maybe you can establish a schedule where you work every morning and have the afternoon off. But consider that many networking events are held in the morning. Perhaps a second shift (3-11 pm) would be advantageous. It leaves your mornings open and should an interview arise, you can set it up for the mornings. Most companies are flexible in scheduling an interview. And this gives you some temporary income while you complete your search. And you may even be able to receive some benefits such as medical insurance with this temporary job.

On one of those days when you do not have anything scheduled, go ahead and take a break and clean out that garage.

You have wanted to do that for the last six months and your excuse was you were too busy. Well, now you're not and once it is done you may find there are enough items that you were going to throw out to have a garage or yard sale. Not only will this kept your mind busy but gives you the opportunity to make some extra cash. You can even get the entire family involved and take this into the house and attic. I have known families that have had yard sales that generated upwards of $1,000 in sales. Tie this into a community yard sale to generate more interest and customers. You might even meet someone who will offer you an employment lead.

Macy's, JC Penney, and Sears are wonderful stores but so are Kmart and Wal-Mart. The biggest difference between these retailers is primarily price. At this point, purchasing that pair of slacks or blouse at one of the upscale retailers for $100 probably prevents you from purchasing 4 or 5 slacks or blouses at the local discount stores. You need not worry about your country club golf partner. You do need to worry about your family who look up to you and expect you to find solutions to this problem. Consider even the possibility of shopping at Goodwill or Salvation Army stores. I have known shoppers who have purchased items there with the original price tags still on them for a substantially lower price. There are Salvation Army and other thrift stores that may be in your neighborhood. If you are concerned that one of your neighbors may see you, visit a store across town. Another source of assistance is your church. Most churches will offer some assistance, depending how large the church is. Smaller churches may not have the funds but have ministry groups that will assist. One of the members of my churches men's club lost his home due to fire and it was pleasing to watch so many people jump in and help. I firmly believe that many people thrive on helping those in need. Would you not help if you were on the other side of the table? Speak with your Pastor and let him know your situation. He can, at the very least, offer some spiritual guidance to you.

During your visit to the state assistance and unemployment offices look into any training and development programs they may have. They are usually free and may give you the opportunity to brush up on your training. Many times the unemployment office will offer courses on Access, Excel and

PowerPoint for free. Perhaps you have never even taken one of these courses, so right now you have the opportunity to take the course and add it to your resume. Your local library may offer free courses along these same lines. This unemployment office most likely even offers assistance on resumes and interviewing. Take advantage of this free advice. Visit the office when you are in the area or look online.

You may have funds available in a 401 plan but be cautious here. The future will come, despite this recent turn of events. Withdrawing funds from 401 plans can be costly. If you are under 59 ½ years of age, there is a 10% penalty plus the normal income tax that will be assessed. Consider the possibility of rolling it over to an IRA if you do not need the money. Of course, this must be done without 60 days. If you can avoid touching these funds, then so be it. You set these plans up for when you retire and that is still going to come some day. Each person's circumstances are different and require a serious look at whether it is feasible to do so or not.

There may be availability of cash advances on your credit cards, assuming you have not exceeded your line of credit. The interest rate on these cash advances can be higher and usually start accruing as soon as you take the advance, unlike normal purchases you make where you will have 25 days from the closing date. Although the interest rate may be high, it may be one of the few alternatives you have. Just put much thought into this and use the credit cards sparingly. You still have to pay it back and your next job may not offer the same salary structure as your previous job. Using these charge cards may become a necessity for something as simple as gasoline for your auto or expenses associated with your job search. Certain memberships in networking events or the purchase of resume paper or printer cartridges could be tax deductible.

Go to the: **http://www.irs.gov/publications/index.html** for further information on forms and publications to assist you. Make sure you keep receipts for all expenditures associated with your job search. You will need these if the expense is an allowable one for job search. Also, keep track of your automobile mileage because this may be a deduction as well. For the 2008 tax year, you were entitled to $0.55 per mile for the first six months of 2008 and $0585 for the remaining six months. Parking and tolls may be deducted in addition. It might be advisable to purchase a small pocket notebook to leave in your vehicle for tracking any expenses. You can purchase ones especially designed for expenses in your local office products store.

Below is a sample table for tracking your expenses.

DATE	EXPENSE	AMOUNT	MILEAGE	COMMENTS
7/01/07	Printer Cartridge	$34.95		Office Depot
7/12/07	Workforce Event		43	Begin 73,111 Ending 73,154
7/1207	Printing of resumes	$10.50		
7/12/07	Postage stamps	$41.00		
7/13/07	Networking Event		57	Begin 73,244 Ending 73,301
7/13/07	Job Fair		32	Begin 73,301 Ending 73,333
7/16/07	Networking Event		20	Begin 73,511 Ending 73,531
7/17/07	Job Fair		50	Begin 73,531 Ending 73,581
7/18/07	Postage	$41.00		
7/23/07	Lunch	$12.50		
7/24/07	Lunch	$ 9.75		
7/25/07	Networking Event		42	Begin 73,745 Ending 73,787
7/26/07	Job Fair		15	Begin 73,787 Ending 73,802
7/27/07	Networking Event		20	Begin 73,802 Ending 73,822
7/30/07	Lunch	$10.50		
7/31/07	Job Fair		30	Begin 73,955 Ending 73,985

I would encourage you to review the following IRS publications for ideas on what tax deductions you can take. You will notice that one of these publications relates to moving expenses. IRS allows, with exceptions, some moving expenses, should the move be necessary for a new job.

Title	Publication Number
Travel, Entertainment, Gifts and Car Expenses	463
Moving Expenses	521
Miscellaneous Expenses	529
Business Expenses	535

    Contact each of your lending institutions and advise them of your situation. Many times they will permit deferments for your monthly payment. For example, on your auto loan with a payment of $350 you may be able to make a deferment in the area of $35-50. Although this is a one-time event, it will give you an extra $300 in your monthly budget. Even your mortgage company may have a plan to assist you, especially if it is a government backed loan such as FHA or VA. They may have a plan where you can get your payments reduced for a specified period of time, normally more than one month. That $1,000 mortgage payment you have could conceivably be reduced by up to 50%. Keep in mind these are approximations, not actual. They may not work with you but you will never know unless you make the phone call. You don't want to lose your home to foreclosure and the bank does not want it so they will most likely do what they can to assist you in this time of need. Of course, any reduction in payments will have to be made up, but it does give you some breathing room. Your lender may also have a program where they can refinance your home and you may be able to draw some equity out. Lenders have programs called No Document loans where income is not verified and if you are a management consultant you do have a job.
    Look into HELOC (Home Equity Line of Credit) loans that serve as second mortgages on the property and do not affect the

first mortgage. Perhaps your first mortgage holder has a program for HELOC loans that are also No Doc loans. It costs nothing for the phone call and if you have lived in your property for a number of years you may be surprised at how much equity you have. Most HELOC lenders have minimal, if any closing costs so it won't be necessary to have to produce cash for closing costs. If you learn ahead of time that you may lose your job, then take out a HELOC loan and do not use any cash until circumstances warrant it. While you are working, you will be able to qualify for a loan much easier, since you have income.

Also look into your IRA's for availability of cash. Converting this will create a tax penalty so think hard about it. Is it necessary to close it out? Are there no other sources for cash at this time? Don't overlook that you still have a future and this will come in handy down the road. Look into any pension plans you have that you may be able to borrow against. Some life insurance policies also offer this benefit. Again, make sure that it is absolutely necessary to cash it out. This will have a major effect on your future financial status. This would only pertain to individual policies that you have, not the group plan you had at your last employer because that probably has been dropped at this time due to your termination. It will not be included in your COBRA policy.

Another source of income is a retirement plan that you may have. The positive aspect of this is that it gives you some needed cash. The negatives are that taxation begins on the acceptance of the check so think again about it before accepting the check. If you are under 59½ there is a 10% penalty with certain exclusions. Look into all of the details before you close it out. There may be a possibility you can borrow on this plan as well. If you have a financial planner this would be a good time to speak with them about all of your financial questions.

Consumer Credit Counseling is a non-profit organization that helps debtors get some relief. They will work with your creditors and get payments reduced for a specified period of time, not just one month. Many creditors will accept pennies on the dollar to prevent the possibility of bankruptcy where they may not receive anything. Your cost will be minimal and will be deducted from your weekly payments to the counseling agency. There are many other companies that offer these services but I caution you to research them carefully. They are not always reputable and there are cases where consumers have paid funds for their services only to see nothing was done.

Obviously there is the alternative of bankruptcy, either Chapter 7 or Chapter 13. With Chapter 7 you can wipe out all of your debts, except your mortgage. Of course there are certain restrictions with this such as you may have to return the collateral on the secured debts. Chapter 13 is where a monthly payment is established based on pennies on the dollar of the remaining balance of the debt. Most creditors would rather this plan be filed because they will get some of their balance back. Both of these methods are severe and require some serious thought because they will remain with you for years. If you get back to work a month after the bankruptcy it may all have been for nothing and yet you will have to live with your decision. Although most attorneys will direct you to what is best, there are some unscrupulous attorneys who will push you into it and there is no turning back. I want to reiterate that this is one of the most serious decisions you will make with your finances so proceed cautiously. Keep in mind that your new employer may have a policy of pulling credit reports on candidates. If you file bankruptcy it will show up on your credit report and could prevent you from being offered a job. These reports are obtained by the company to determine how you handle your financial affairs, especially if you are applying for a position in the financial arena or a department that would involve your handling of company funds. So, sit down and put some serious thought into whether bankruptcy, Chapter 7 or 13, is the right way for you to go.

"Don't limit investing to the financial world. Invest something of yourself, and you will be richly rewarded."

-Charles Schwab

5.

RESUMES

NOW IT IS TIME TO GIFT-WRAP YOURSELF. ISN'T THAT WHAT A resume really is…nothing more than gift-wrap for yourself? If you were wrapping a gift for your spouse wouldn't you want it to look as nice as possible? You do not want to bore them with the resume. You need and want to capture their interest, and fast. I once heard someone compare a resume to a movie trailer and that is a good thought. Doesn't presentation usually account for half the battle? There is an old saying that presentation is everything. Remember that you are the product. Any manufacturer will make a tremendous amount of effort to produce a package that makes their actual product as appealing as possible. A resume is like a sales brochure. The last time you booked a trip thru a travel agent and they gave you the travel brochure, was it not appealing enough to get you to dream about the trip? You may have had the desire to go to Maui but once you looked at the brochure it just brought even more anxiety to you. Once you complete the resume, take a look at it as if it were someone you were hiring. Is the resume hitting home? How would the reader accept it? You will know how good it is by how many interviews you are getting. If you are not getting interviews then perhaps the resume is the reason. That's what you want to do to the recruiter; create that same anxiety. This chapter will focus on what it takes to put your qualifications on paper.

When a recruiter looks at a resume, they take less than 60 seconds before they move on to the next one and you need to grab their attention as quickly as possible. You want to showcase your high points so that they will hold it longer than 60 seconds. By having the recruiter holding it more than 60 seconds you are substantially increasing the odds of obtaining an interview. What I want to mention up front is that do not assume you are the world's greatest speller. Do not hesitate to use spell check on your computer. Having spelling and grammatical errors on your resume will reduce the opportunities of it going any further. In addition, once you have completed the resume have someone close to you review it for punctuation and other errors. Spell check may not always pick up on your mistakes. For example, instead of entering "I excelled in areas <u>where</u> the company directed their goals" you actually put "I excelled in areas <u>wear</u> the company directed their goals". See how it changes the picture. Two or three errors like this would give an unfavorable impression of you. Having a member of your management team proof read it should help to locate these types of errors.

Your resume should be one to two pages long. Making it any longer than that may have a tendency to bore the reader and they lose interest in you. I have had so many recruiters tell me that the resume must catch their eye within the first 60 seconds or they will not continue with it. Many times one page will suffice. For example, if your last two jobs accounted for 15 years, then one page will probably prove sufficient. In rare cases, it may be permissible to go to three pages such as in the case of some IT professionals. Make sure the resume is neat and on a good bond paper, preferably 20 lbs. You can tell good bond paper as you can see the bond marking on it. Make sure you have the bond markings right side up before you print the resume on it. It may not get noticed if you do but rest assuredly that if you don't it will get noticed and the reader may have the perception you are not detail oriented. Don't use any color other than white or ivory, as some scanners will not accept colored paper. Purchasing inexpensive flimsy paper may not do justice to all of your quailfications. Spend the extra pennies and have it look professional.

The format should be equally professional. A ten or twelve font in Arial or Times New Roman is appropriate with narrow margins on the side. I remember one resume I developed had margins that were wide and once I completed a second one with less indentation (1"), it looked considerably more professional. In addition, it gave me more opportunity to list additional skills that hopefully grabbed the reader's attention for a longer period of time. As I stated above, the longer they look at it, the more intrigued they will become and that is what gets interviews. Do you think that if the movie previews for a Harry Potter film showed Harry just walking around the castle that would grab the viewer's attention? No, what they show is Harry flying around on a broom or other action packed scenes.

Before you put the resume together, take some time and do a brief outline. First, list all of the dates of your employment and be especially cautious that the dates all match. I have looked at resumes where the dates overlapped each other and made little sense. For example, if you were a loan underwriter from December 2002 through January of 2007 in Richmond, Virginia and the next job you listed was as a loan servicing supervisor from December of 2005 to June of 2009 in Dallas, Texas, something appears wrong here. How could you be in Richmond <u>and</u> Dallas from 12/05 to 2/07? Now there might be a solid explanation but be prepared to explain it. Don't list the explanation on the resume.

Also, for periods of unemployment, it is not necessary to list them on the resume, but then, of course you will have to provide an explanation for it as well on the company application. It is also necessary to only list ten years experience. If your last job was for 5 years and the previous one was 6 years that should be sufficient. Of course if you have been at the same job for 18, years obviously show the entire dates employed. Make sure you keep your resume current, even if you obtain a new position. It is much easier to add a job to an existing resume rather than have to start at scratch again. Your resume will change over time especially as you become more focused on it.

By spending time putting notes together it may help you decide what type of position you really want. I spoke with a career counselor once who said now is the appropriate time to decide "what you want to be when you grow up." After you assemble the dates, list all of your qualifications. This will prove to be a vital part of the resume and should be listed somewhere near the top third of the resume. These can be single words that give a good snapshot of your qualifications. Next, put some notes together that indicate what you did for each employer. When you put the resume together it won't be necessary to have long sentences. Just a few intelligent words can say a lot about what you did. Think back over your entire career with each company. Watch that you are not overly boastful, list only factual information.

Although the resume is a marketing tool, don't be one of those who fall in the category of thinking they are perfect and conquered the world. You will turn the reader off and lose any chance of obtaining an interview. Your resume should only give the basics of what you have accomplished in your recent career. As you list all of your many qualifications watch for the occupational phrases or jargon that may confuse the reader. Try to make sure that anyone without any knowledge of your industry will be able to thoroughly understand your resume. In some cases, such as the technology world, it is not always possible but this is understood. And remember the recruiter is not going to read your resume word for word. They will initially scan it taking not more than 60 seconds. If you are a viable candidate, then they will look further into the resume.

Action verbs should be placed throughout the resume to give it a feel of excitement and accomplishment. Below is just a sample of some commonly used action verbs. They may also help you to remember what you did for each employer and once listed on the resume it will come to life.

accelerated	directed	persuaded
accomplished	distributed	prepared
achieved	drafted	processed
acquired	engineered	programmed
adapted	established	promoted
administered	evaluated	proposed
advanced	expanded	published
alleviated	facilitated	recorded
analyzed	formulated	recruited
budgeted	generated	reduced
built	implemented	refined
centralized	improved	reorganized
coached	increased	reproduced
collaborated	initiated	requisitioned
commanded	instituted	researched
communicated	integrated	resolved
compiled	invented	restructured
conducted	launched	revised
constructed	lead	solved
consulted	managed	streamlined

There are companies that will create a professional looking resume for you at a considerable cost. Costs can range from $200 to $1000. I am not advising you that one way or the other is better but I would encourage you to attempt creating one yourself initially. The cost of a professional resume may not fit into your budget and with a little reading at your local library and some quiet time, I am confident you can effectively develop a very professional looking resume. If you decide to have it professionally done you can go online and find many companies that will do this for you.

However, if you decide to give it a shot yourself, visit your local library and you will see an abundance of books on resume writing. There are also resume-blasting companies that you can hire to mass mail your resume. Again, there is a cost involved and you need to think about the pros and cons of doing this. If you hire a company to blast your resume you are adding an additional cost that may crimp your wallet. You must consider the fact that your resume may be sent to companies that either do not provide a good fit for you or companies that you would be adverse to work for. In addition, some companies discard unsolicited resumes so you could be wasting your money.

Your resume would not necessarily be worded to provide the best introduction of your qualifications. Resumes should be worded to fit the particular position you are applying for. I personally do not feel generic resumes provide the job searcher the best punch for the dollar, so to speak. You want to be able to fit your resume to the position you are applying for. This will provide the reader a greater feel for who you are and what you are looking for. Some career counselors will advise you not to send out unsolicited resumes and to target only those jobs that you are qualified for. This makes good sense and avoids wasted time.

With the advent of technology playing a larger part in today's society, many companies use scanning systems (ATS) to review their resumes. These scanning systems look for key words that are part of the job description for the vacant position. Your generic resume may not have these key words. By looking at the posted job description you can locate the key words and insert them in your resume. Certainly I am not advising you to fabricate anything, but too often I have seen jobs that I felt qualified for due to past experience but my wording may not have given the recruiter the same feeling. This scanning system is used to filter out resumes, not to hire a candidate. Once the field is narrowed down then the hiring process can start. Many times when I reviewed applications as a hiring manager I would see resumes that were so far off base in the qualifications for the job that I wondered what this person was thinking. Obviously the positive thing about resume blasting companies is that they can send out more resumes in a shorter time than you can. Again, this is a personal decision that only you can make. There are some very reputable companies out there that perform this task. If you decide to go this route, just do some simple research to locate the best company for you. One other note here is not to "dumb down" the resume. If you have the skill, list it. Your experience is what it is. In the long run this may assist in getting you a more senior position, one that is more compatible with your skills.

Although we will get into the organization of the resume later in this chapter, I feel it is appropriate to discuss some common sense issues about developing your resume. First and foremost, do not ever lie or fabricate anything on your resume. These lies will come out eventually, whether it is before you get the interview or after you get the job. Why jeopardize a good opportunity that you may be qualified for in hopes of getting that interview. I remember one time a friend of mine applied for a job implying on the resume he had a four-year degree, although he did not. He did not list a graduation date but did list the college and years he attended. Once he got the interview he then listed on the employment application that in fact he did have a degree. He got the job and the company moved him a considerable distance and paid all moving costs. Two weeks into the job he was summoned to the human resources office and when confronted with the lie, he admitted he had exaggerated his education. The company immediately terminated him and in addition he was required to reimburse the company for the moving costs. Now he was out of work in a new area, with a large expense to reimburse and a family waiting for him to solve this dilemma. The sad part was that the company indicated they would have hired him even without the degree.

Make sure your facts are just that with, no fluff intertwined. However, do not get carried away in the other direction. Do not hesitate to brag about your accomplishments. If you won awards, list them. If you accomplished something special for the company, such as saving the company a large amount of money on a new procedure, list it. If you don't brag about yourself who else is going to do it? Do not feel it is necessary to defend yourself with your resume. Here again, list the facts and be proud of what you have accomplished. It is not uncommon for a human resources department to receive in excess of 500 resumes for one position. With this in mind, you must differentiate yourself from the rest. These employers are extremely busy and their time is valuable, so do what you can to make their job easier. By having an accurate, factual resume you will be giving the employer a true picture of yourself. Have confidence that your qualifications will get you that interview. Making sure that the resume is accurate will help the employer to know what your qualifications are and whether you are a good fit for the position based on initial findings. Of course, the interview will provide the true picture but it is the goal of the resume to get the interview not the job. At that point your other skills will kick in.

There are two types of resumes: chronological and functional. You will see examples of both later in the chapter. A chronological resume, which is the most popular, keys in on your dates of employment and basically brags about your longevity in each position, and will emphasize your job stability. It will list work experience with the most recent employment first. If for any reason your career has been marked by constant job turnover and gaps in employment, then perhaps the functional resume is best suited to you. Having gaps on a resume creates red flags and the functional resume helps you avoid this. College graduates will be more successful using a functional resume. A functional resume emphasizes what you have accomplished rather than focusing on the dates. It emphasizes your knowledge, skills and attributes. Although recruiters are not fond of functional resumes, you may need it to get to the next level.

Having been at the wrong end of several mergers and buyouts late in my career, there were several gaps in my employment. Initially I used the chronological resume, however it produced few results. At that point I refined it and used a combination of a chronological and functional resume to get my point across. By doing this it provided much more success. A resume is just a tool that will provide the reader with a silent history of what you have done, your skills and qualifications, as well as what experience you have to offer. Military experience need not be listed on either resume unless it provides relevant experience to the position you are applying for or falls into the necessary chronological period. For example if you spent 4 years in the Air Force and your job was to program computers and this is what you are looking to do in the civilian world then, by all means list it. If it occurred 20 years ago though, it will not serve much purpose. The reader will determine that those skills you used are out dated now and no longer relevant to the position you are applying for. Now, if you were a tank driver in the Army and you are applying for an accounting position, leave the military experience off, unless it creates a gap.

Once you have completed your resume take advantage of the posting service that many job search web sites offer. For example Monster and CareerBuilder both allow you to store up to five resumes. You can create several different resumes that are slightly different and may not work for similar positions. For example, let's say you are in the collections field and you have worked for banks or finance companies. You may want one resume to apply for positions with either of these types of companies. Yet, perhaps you have call center experience in your background, so that resume may be slightly different and you want to target call center operations. There is no fee to do this and there certainly can be a great advantage to having several different resumes posted. What you also want to do is go in monthly and make some kind of adjustment to each. The reason for this is that recruiters look at the new resumes posted and if you make any kind of adjustment then it will appear to them as a new one posted. For example, you can add or eliminate your middle initial and alternate monthly. Take advantage of every opportunity you have to get your resume in the hands of recruiters and those making the hiring decisions.

One area of the resume that has concerned me is the email addresses that job applicant's list. It does not make sense to apply for a professional position and your email address is less than professional. Having johnsbeerbelly@isp.com will undoubtedly turn a recruiter off. I have seen other instances where the email address was even somewhat provocative. Forget having any recruiter attempt to contact you. How can a company expect this applicant to be professional when their resume is less than such? Take the time to create a second email address for job search purposes. I had one friend who used something similar to johnssearch@network.com (rather than his personal email) as the email address specifically for his job search. Most ISP's will allow you to have more than one email address for free. Take advantage of this so as not to miss out on that special career opportunity. Cell phone numbers are optional on a resume.

If you are in the position of considering a career change then a good source may be www.online.onetcenter.org. This site may provide some answers or direction on your career change. You can find occupations using keywords. Perhaps you have a skill or certain knowledge and you want to know what other careers are available using this knowledge. You can also use acronyms and pull up matching careers. You can also pull up labor market information for your particular state. Just Google the state and list labor market information. For example: Florida labor market information will give you more demographics than you could dream of. If you are looking for information on salaries to determine if a particular occupational field is right for you go to www.salary.com. You can enter a job title and zip code and get salary information for that particular occupation. I pulled up Project Manager for Construction and found that the range was from \$53,279 to \$94,677 with a 75th percentile at \$85,037.

Let's discuss the format of a resume beginning with the heading. The heading should include the following:

- Name: should be in bold letters. Let your name stand out.
- Address: make sure it is complete and no spelling errors such as in the name of the street.
- Contact numbers: both your home and cell phone numbers. Give the recruiter every opportunity to contact you.
- Email address: make sure it is spelled correctly. This is another means of contact and obviously it should be a professional email address as discussed previously, but is optional to list.

The heading is what is going to stand out to any recruiter that pulls up your resume so it should look professional and be accurate. I remember looking at a friend's resume and as he was telling me how he had just sent it out to all of the recruiters in his field within the state. I noticed his phone number had a typographical error in it and his cell phone was not listed. Do you think he got any contacts from that resume? He not only wasted a lot of time but it also raised some concern to any recruiter that tried calling him. I might add that his resume, other than the telephone number typo, was excellent and warranted recruiters to go the next step, yet they could not. They may email him but they certainly are not going to take the time to postal mail him. That may have cost him a prime job.

The next section is a matter of preference. Many resumes I have seen list Objective as the next section. You would list what your career objective is as it pertains to the particular company you are applying to. It could be standard and never fluctuate but if you are considering more than one career, it should have some flexibility. There is some thought in the career field that listing the candidates objective is passé. As recruiters are so busy and only spend 60 seconds looking at the resume, why waste valuable time with your objective when it probably won't make a difference to the recruiter. Perhaps you can list the objective on one of your stored resumes and leave it off of the next and monitor the results on each. My preference is not to list the objective. If you are going to list the objective here might be one example of what you could list:

"To obtain a position with a progressive company that values employee dedication and loyalty as well as providing a strong customer service based atmosphere."

The next section would be Experience. List here what you have done over the last 10 years. List the company name, preferably in bold lettering along with the location. For example, **THE ABC COMPANY**, Orlando, FL. I used a 14 font for the company name and a 12 font for the location. That way it stands out and if you have worked for a major U.S. company such as IBM or Bank of America, it will grab the reader's eye quicker. To the far right list the dates you were employed. For many years it was normal to list the month and year yet there has been a more recent trend to just list the years. Below the company name list your position with the company. It might have been Vice President of Manufacturing or Regional Sales Manager. Now what follows is a matter of preference and if you asked ten individuals you would get a good mix of opinions.

Many people simply go right into their responsibilities in shortened sentences such as the examples below:

Sales manager of 20-person sales force with responsibilities for business development in the pool supply business. Produced $1,000,000 in sales three years running and received Sales Person of the Year twice. Developed new marketing program.

Developed new software program to be used in national marketing program. Recognized for improvements to existing software program being awarded Creative Design of the Year award. Oversee project team responsible for $2,000,000 annual budget.

Responsible for opening new call center operation for 110 person inbound center. Exceeded company goal of directing the center to be operational in 90 days. Received Customer Service Person of the Year award, given to top manager.

These are just three samples of how you can describe your positions. One other suggestion would be to provide as many numbers as possible and bold them so they also stand out such as "reduced expense rations by **17%**." See how the boldness immediately grabs your eye. If you list two or three with each job description then when the reader picks up the resume they will have a tendency to focus on all of these accomplishments.

Another thought to listing job descriptions is using bullet points rather than the sentences. One human resource executive I recently spoke with stated that bullets look crisper and are easier on the eye giving the reader more of your qualifications in a shorter period of time.

- Produced **$2,000,000** in annual revenue
- Reduced expenses by **22%**
- Produced **$1,000,000** in sales last year receiving Salesman of Year award

See how you can say just as much with less wording and perhaps create some interest to the reader. Most recruiters do not want to read wordy resumes especially if they have to look at 200 resumes for the advertised position. Again, this is a matter of preference. You will also notice there are no periods after bullet entries. Try having a resume set up with each method and see which draws the most attention. Before you send the resume, print out the advertised job description and high-light any key words in the job description and insert them into your text. For example, if the job description lists a job need of "perform excel spreadsheet calculations" then, assuming you know excel, list these words in one of your job descriptions. If there is a scanning system used, then it will pick up on this. Do this as often as possible. Just make sure that your expertise is obvious and not confusing to the reader. The reader may just be a recruiter who does not know what the AS400 system is, etc.

The next section on the resume is education. All you need to do here is list the degree, college name and GPA. Do not list the date you graduated as this will alert the reader as to your age and if you are older such as a baby boomer, this may create some concern on the recruiting side. We all know that age discrimination is illegal but it does exist in the work place. You may be forwarding your resume to a thirty-year-old MBA who could feel intimidated by you. Don't give them that opportunity until you are able to defend yourself at an interview. Get the interview first! That is your goal with the resume…not to get eliminated needlessly. This will take some effort but it can be accomplished.

There is some thought in the career search field that if you have an MBA then it may not always be a good choice to list it. My thought is that you should always list it. Education should be an indication of your accomplishments, and the competition is overwhelming now. The last section will list any certifications or licenses you have that are relevant to the position. I would suggest you do not list any certifications or licenses that are not relevant. This leaves open an opportunity to question why you have them. Several years ago you would find many resumes listing hobbies and sometimes gender. Do not, under any circumstances list hobbies, gender, age, social security numbers, graduation dates or "personal references upon request". Nor would you list any personal references. If these references are needed, the company will ask for them at the appropriate time.

Make sure your writing is not flamboyant or overly creative. As I stated previously, recruiters "want just the facts, ma'am, just the facts" as Joe Friday on Dragnet used to say. Don't provide any opportunities to file your resume away too quickly. You could also list career affiliations that you are associated with. Some of these might be trade organizations or volunteering. Mentioned earlier was that you should only have 1 or 2 pages listing approximately 10 years experience. Do not feel you must list all 25 years experience, as that also will date you. Listing only 10 years experience makes it difficult for the reader to identify your age. Besides, what you did 25 years ago has little bearing on what you can do now or what the position requires. Just think how much has changed in your profession in just the last 10 years, never mind 20 or 25 years. So there is no advantage and possibly a disadvantage to listing more than 10 years. Once you get into the interview you can also put a positive spin should the discussion lead toward your 25 years experience. Now, if you have been with your last employer for 20 or 25 years, then you cannot help the experience part but having that much experience with the same company will most likely offset everything else. It will give a great view of your job stability.

As you prepare the body of the resume, you must keep in mind that you are possibly just one of 200+ candidates submitting resumes for the position. You need to take every possibility of shining above the rest. Show all of your accomplishments, with the greatest or most impressive first. This might be where you saved one of your previous employers a large amount of money on a project or that you won salesman of the year. Perhaps you were responsible for $1,000,000 in sales or that you led a team of 250, winning customer service awards. Make sure these greatnesses include numbers or percentages. These types of entries stand out and will grab the attention of the reader and are in essence the punch line of the resume. Although sometimes difficult, bragging is necessary.

Don't miss any opportunities to stand out from the rest; however do not lose sight of the employers needs. If you have affiliations that are representative of your career, list them. If you bowl in your church league, leave it off. Cater your resume to convince the employer you are the best candidate. This should be accomplished by dissecting the job description. If you have previous military experience look for jobs you performed in the military to tie into the resume. You may have taken leadership courses that would dress up the resume. But keep the resume flowing and easy to read. You don't want to be showing talents for the sales job you are applying for and mentioning that you were a tank driver in the military. There has to be some connection from your past duties or responsibilities and the new job description. The recruiter must be able to understand what you did at your previous employer.

Here is an example of a good and bad notation:

> Bad: Led a call center group.
> Good: Directed an inbound call center team of 150, winning three customer service awards and improving employee retention by 12%.

Which one of these candidates would you want to hire? The bad job description is just another apple in the bushel whereas the good description is the big, red apple on top of the bushel. Don't make these job descriptions too long by going on and on and not saying anything. Recruiters want short, crisp comments. I caution you again that only deal with the facts….no fabrications. These will be easily found out and you could be worse off than when you initially started the process for this position. Your integrity will be questioned and perhaps accepting this position and losing it days or weeks later will create a greater hardship.

When you initially begin the resume, concentrate on the top third of the page. Imagine the resume folded in thirds and the recruiter will only see one-third of the resume. Direct your strongest efforts here, especially with your greatnesses. I mention the top third because that is probably all the recruiter will see of your resume unless you convince him or her to look further. Remember that the first 30 seconds the recruiter is looking at your resume is the most crucial. Some candidates list their objective in the top third of the resume; however I again suggest that you eliminate this. The employer does not care about your objective but only what they want out of a candidate to fill their position. If you really feel it is necessary then cater it to the position that is being advertised.

During your search process, as you see the positions you want, there will be occasions where you actually will have to complete an online application even before the interview takes place. Make sure you complete this application in its entirety. Omitting information could have a negative effect on your chances to get that interview. The recruiters are looking for as much information as possible and the information you think is not important may be just what the employer is looking for. This brings up some necessary caution regarding your resume. Once you have put it all together, use spell check. One little typo or misplaced word says a lot. The recruiter may label you as one who cannot spell and question why you did not at least take the extra few seconds to use your computers spell check. Not only will they think you can't spell, but that you do not care enough to take the time to use spell check. You must consistently polish and refine your resume. Proofread the entire resume and let your significant other or someone from your management team proofread it as well. Another pair of eyes may give a different perspective, not so much for spelling but to determine whether the resume makes sense and determine whether the words are flowing smoothly and properly.

Just remember one other thing…rewrite, rewrite, and rewrite. Don't hesitate about having more than one resume saved in your database. Have a couple slightly different resumes so you can gear these to different positions that you may be interested in. For example, maybe have one that is geared toward you being a sales rep while the other one is geared towards VP of Marketing. This will save you time when you have to submit a resume and possibly avoid sending one that does not meet the objectives of the position in regards to the job description.

Once you have submitted your resume for a particular position don't just sit back and wait for the employer to call you. That may not happen, yet you could be a viable candidate. Wait several days and follow up with the recruiter. Call them and verify they have received your resume and question the time element of the process. Ask them how soon they will start conducting interviews. This may be an opportunity for a short telephone interview to get you moved to the next step in the process. Think of how a funnel works with the top being the widest. The top of the funnel is the initial resume recruiting process. As the funnel flows downward so do the resumes. Less and less make it down the spout. You must be persistent in the process and maybe a second phone call will be necessary. I do strongly caution you to not stalk the recruiter, as that will be the quickest way to get eliminated. I have found that many recruiters know what the job descriptions states and if they do not see this exactly in your resume they will go on to the next one. They may not even understand what the position really is and yet you do have the experience in the field. Keep this in mind as you prepare your resume for this position.

During my search process I came across several career counselors that felt you should not send your resume out blindly and that you must establish target companies. I do not agree with this assumption. What if the company did not currently have a position open and once they saw your qualifications they then considered creating a position? I have known several candidates that had this happen to them. One acquaintance I met at a networking event told me how they attended a job fair and while speaking to a recruiter that the recruiter was so impressed that they openly stated they must bring this candidate onboard and that they were going to go back to their office and discuss it with the HR manager. As of the writing of this text, a position was in the process of being created.

Now I would emphasize here that you should only send resumes to companies blindly that could use your qualifications. Sending your resume to every company in a professional park is not only a waste of time but expensive as well. Stick to the companies that specialize in your area of expertise. For example, if you are a loan officer, contact every mortgage company and bank in your vicinity. It is a good idea to create a target list of companies to concentrate on. Know who the key hiring people are in these companies and direct your efforts to them, and not blindly to the Human Resources department. If you don't know who they are, then take a minute and call the company and ask.

Most of the time someone at the company will most likely tell you who the VP is of that particular department. If not, then call back and ask for the purchasing department and when they answer just say you are sorry but that you were supposed to be transferred to the VP of Marketing, etc. They won't ask questions and will transfer you to that person. When you blindly send out a resume, try to forward it to a key person in the organization, preferably the most senior person. When you send it to the President of XYZ Corporation he will probably forward it to human resources. Assume you were the recipient of that resume from the president of the company, what would you do with it? You would undoubtedly make every attempt to contact that person who submitted the resume.

When you do send it by email, put your name on the subject line along with resume. That gives you further identification by name recognition. If you do not have that persons email address try to locate anyone's email address in that company and you can most likely come up with the correct one. For example if you know John Jones in accounting and his email address is jjones@xyz.com then you can assume that the president will be in the same format. Also, many company websites list the officers of the company and sometimes even the email address. Use your local telephone book to locate companies in your respective field. In addition, the library can be an excellent resource. Business journals throughout Florida offer The Book of Lists, which you can either purchase or obtain free with the newspaper subscription or even view it at the library. It lists all of the major companies in your area for particular fields. It includes manufacturing companies, banks, credit unions, recruiting companies, etc.

If you answer an advertisement with a resume and they want your salary expectations, this usually causes a dilemma. You are hesitant about being pigeon holed with regards to your salary requirements and creating less of an opportunity for negotiating at a later time. My suggestion is to ignore this question and move on. You are taking a chance of being excluded, but consider that if you list your salary requirements you may get eliminated anyway. This just depends on how bad you want to get into this company. If it is one of your target companies high on your list, you may be more flexible in salary requirements so go ahead and list your desired salary. Also, if you know what the salary range is at the company from former employees, then you are able to list some figure. Some systems that ask for salary requirements may accept any digit such as $1.00. If that works, then you may have bypassed the question for the time being. If it doesn't then you may have to list your salary requirements. Be prepares for this and determine what your range is prior to getting to this point.

If you are mailing resumes, which is rare in this technology savvy world, make sure it is on a good white or ivory paper. Do not use pastels as that will not impress the reader and there is the chance they could discard it because of its color. And as we stated previously, many scanners do not accept colored paper. There is new technology advancement in resume production and that is video resumes or resumes on CD. Although we are in a technology savvy world many recruiters are too busy and they will not take the time to look at this form of submission. You are wasting your time, expense and chances of getting that interview. In fact, they may not even have a way to review it. This submission may also come across as being flamboyant. In addition, it's too long to grab their attention. Now, if you have been recruited and they request your resume you may be in a better situation to use the resume CD. These CD's are a great resource if used appropriately.

Another source of producing resumes is hiring professional resume writers to develop your resume. The cost of this can run from $200 to over $1000. The only thing I caution you here about is if you are going to use this source make sure they are professional and not just someone like you or your neighbor writing your resume. Many times a recruiter will take up a part time job of writing resumes with no formal training. If they can't provide before and after samples then maybe you are barking up the wrong tree. Don't waste your money. Look for referrals of professional resume writers so that you will get your money's worth. There are many great companies out there that will produce an excellent resume.

In this next section we will discuss cover letters. Many times cover letters are not even an option. Submitting resumes online often do not allow you to send cover letters and that is fine. There are also some recruiters who do not even look at cover letters. When I was hiring someone I never looked at cover letters. I would find that everything I needed to know was in the resume and if it was not, most likely the cover letter was not going to enlighten me at all. Now, here again there are some career counselors who feel cover letters are very important. Use your discretion here and proceed with your gut feeling. It most likely will be correct. If you decide to use a cover letter, keep it to two or three paragraphs. Use this space to key in on your major skills and attributes. Appeal to the readers needs by demonstrating how you will fit into these needs.

If you are mailing a resume, then you should send a cover letter because the recipient does not know what you are applying for. If you are emailing a resume you should also send a short email describing what you are looking for. You have to send the email with your resume so why not list a few opening comments. Whenever you do send a cover letter, keep it short and sweet. Hit on the high points and move on because that is what the reader is going to do. Direct your comments to how you can solve the company's need as we discussed. Focus on your knowledge, skills and attributes but briefly and with clarity. Make sure if you are mailing it that it is typed and neat. Never handwrite a cover letter as it lacks any professionalism. Cover letters are used to direct the attention of the reader to the high points or assets of the resume. Make it clear as to why you are sending the resume. Mention what position or positions you are looking for. It should not be any longer than two to three paragraphs so just focus on the main points. Make sure you proofread it before you mail it. Also, be professional in your salutation such as using Mr. or Mrs. and never just the first name. Another format you could use is known as the T style. What you would do here is list the company's needs on the left and how you can fulfill them on the right.

See the example below.

Company Needs	My Qualifications
College Degree required	BS in Manufacturing
3 years experience	12 years in Manufacturing
Computer knowledge	Excel and Microsoft Office

Keep in mind that you want your cover letter to not rehash your resume. It should be brief and to the point hitting on those issues the company is looking for. You want the cover letter to entice the reader to continue on reading the resume. Make your writing interesting but not wild and flashy. You are not going to make this two pages long so be quick and to the point. The first paragraph should contain a "wow" statement to grab the reader's attention immediately. This paragraph should be used to provide the reader a synopsis of what value you would bring to them

The next paragraph should emphasize the first paragraph. You may want to discuss something recent that stands out in your career. You want to show the reader what you can do for them.

The third paragraph should provide further details about your past accomplishments, emphasizing those accomplishments that would be similar to the position you are applying for. It should also summarize everything in no more than three sentences. In this paragraph inform the reader that you will follow up with them at a set time. That way they will be expecting you and most probably have some questions for you. Each sentence must be concise and state your objective persuasively. You only want to emphasize those qualities that directly relate to what the reader desires in the position. Remember, not only is the cover letter used to get the reader to want to look at your resume but to assist you in landing that interview.

During my career search I kept a detailed notebook listing several different items. I kept a list of all companies that I forwarded resumes to whether they were recruiters, blind ad companies or companies that advertised positions. In addition, I also kept a copy of the job description or job advertisement. That way, when I spoke with a recruiter about the position, I had all of the facts right before me. Just before an interview I could brush up on the job description and requirements so that I could mention key phrases during the interview. There was also a section that listed all of the expenses associated with my job search so I could use these for income tax deductions. Noted with these expenses was the individual mileage for trips to networking events or job interviews. The need to be organized during your job search is extremely important.

Having a current calendar in this notebook gave me the opportunity to plan a month in advance that way there were no missed opportunities. I also keep all of the business cards I obtained from networking events, etc. in a clear sheet so that I could refer back to them. I made it a habit of weekly sending emails touching base with others and this provided an excellent source for me. I had all of the material right at hand. It kept me in line with all of the items I listed

"Armed with the knowledge of our past, we can with confidence charter a course for our future."

-Malcolm X

John Doe

123 Elm St. (603) 123-4567
Any town, USA 67890
john@aol.com

Expertise

Marketing Director: Highly successful marketing professional knowledgeable in consumer products and commercial chemicals. Experienced in product branding and strategic marketing research.

Experience:

ABC Marketing Corp. Boston, Mass., Marketing Director (May 2004-present)
- Led western division in sales from 2004-2006
- Won Salesman of the Year award, 2005 & 2006
- Developed new marketing strategy, implemented throughout company

Crosby Consumer Sales, Lowell, Mass., Marketing Rep (Nov. 2001-May 2004)
- Producer of record sales for packaged goods, 2002 & 2003
- Created national sales campaign resulting in $2,000,000 new business
- Supervised sales administrative staff

Manda Chemical Corp., Boston, Mass., Marketing Director (Feb 1992-Nov.2001)
- Implemented marketing training manual for new employees
- Managed a team of 9 sales representatives
- Created partnerships with 5 global companies

Education:

University of New Hampshire, Durham, N.H.
    Bachelors Degree, Marketing, 3.5 GPA

Affiliations:

National Sales and Marketing Committee (2002-2006)
U. S. Association of Marketing Executives (2000-2006)
Chicago Assoc.of Marketing Representatives (1998-2002)

Mary Smith

890 Cranberry St. (352) 456-7890
Any town, USA 65432 mary@anytown.com

Qualifications:

Senior level marketing executive proficient and adept at communicating with all levels of management. Knowledgeable in consumer recreational products, strategic marketing plans, and innovative sales plans.

Experience:

Rapid Sales Corp., Raleigh, N.C., Marketing Director
2000-2007

Developed international marketing campaign and designed strategic plan for implementing program. Led 12 member marketing team for western division and receiving National Salesman of Year award two consecutive years. Produced five years of sales in excess of $1,000,000.

Crest Marketing Grp, Durham, N.C., Marketing Director
1995-2000

Designed innovative marketing program for staff of 10. Received recognition for outstanding sales for multimedia programs. Implemented team building strategies which assisted in creating 5 consecutive years of improved sales. Developed new program for training sales reps resulting in improved employee retention.

Education:

University of Southern California, Los Angeles, CA.
 B.S. in Marketing-4.0 GPA
 MBA-4.0

Paul Parker

17 Elm St. (915) 223-6655
Any town, USA 48979 paul@email.com

Summary: Results oriented leader experience marketing and product management. Experienced in supervising teams of up to 350 employees. Six Sigma knowledge.

Experience:

Random Marketing Corp., Orlando, FL
Operations Manager 2001-2007

Led team of 350 call center sales associates specializing in consumer products, earning recognition for leading company in software sales. Set company record for employee retention at 9%.

Auto Remarketing of America, Daytona, FL
Operations Manager 1996-2001

Developed marketing programs for sale of automobile detailing products for national sales program. Received 1997 and 2000 Customer Service Excellence awards. Implemented new software program for call center producing $1,500,000 annual sales.

Carlson Software Corp., Orlando, FL
Operations Manager 1989-1996

Directed 100 member sales force selling computer software products. Received recognition for implementing new marketing program 3 months ahead of target. Responsible for long range planning and budgeting of company sales division.

Education
University of N. C.
    B.S. in Business Management-3.94 GPA

LOUISE RAND
123 Oak St. PalmSprings,34554 (455) 123-4555 lour@isp.com

Passionate driver with diverse background in leadership and management, credit and collections, as well as vendor management and call center operations. Performance based manager recognized as a cross functional team builder while performing as strong promoter of staff development for creating and executing outstanding customer service. Knowledgeable in financial services for lending products as well as ancillary insurance products. Extremely effective at implementing a tangible and result-oriented "outrageous customer service" approach in operations. Demonstrates a high degree of integrity with exceptional staffing, training, process improvement and P&L skills.

LEADERSHIP & MANAGEMENT

- Maintained being in the top 20% of the company in 2006 with 32% profit margin.
- Reduced employee turnover by 25% utilizing self developed training systems, recognition programs and the redesign of hiring processes which increased productivity by 35% leading to over 5% reduction in delinquency.
- Led company in revenue production of $1,000,000 for 7 consecutive months along with maintaining the lowest expense ratio.
- Directed 15 branch multi-unit full service lending operation.
- Led 2 teams with over 400 FTE and contracted employees.
- Established employee training programs, performance evaluations and business plans.
- Conducted client presentations and business development strategies.

PROFESSIONAL EXPERIENCE

VP Collections **Super Collections Agency 2004-2007**
- Sub-prime automobile collections operation to include bankruptcy and recovery.
- Led team consisting of 3 divisions in inbound/outbound call center operation.
- Primarily responsible for customer service and delinquency control.

VP Operations, **Horizon Collection Systems 2001-2004**
- Mortgage servicing for collections.
- Consulted to independent insurance and mortgage companies.
- Serviced $110 million in collection receivables.

Director, **Crystal Bank 1998-2001**
- Led real estate department in overseeing collections.
- Drove mortgage collections to all time company low of 1%.
- Directed team of over 100 full time employees.

EDUCATION & CERTIFICATIONS

BS in Organizational Management,
Columbus University, Sacramento, CA. 3.94 GPA

RALPH JONES

789 Crestview Dr.   (941) 678-9876
Valley View, FL. 32546   rj@aol.com

Professional Summary

Ten years experience with financial services, compliance and reprocessing. Documented records of improving process systems and procedures. Experienced in implementing project enhancements.

Cary Financial Services Director of Compliance
                                             Memphis, Tenn.
                                                     2005-2009

- Responsible for all compliance issues in multi faceted financial services operation
- Redesigned company procedures manual for field compliance issues
- Reduced compliance issues by 33%

Staten Design Systems Vice President of Processing
                                               Knoxville, Tenn.
                                                     2001-2005

- Implemented company-wide system for financial services compliance
- Created company procedures manual
- Designed benefits program for human resources department

Vector Design Corp. Director of Processing
                                                Clarksville, Tenn.
                                                     1995-2001

- Restructured credit card processing design
- Led company in revenue generation
- Implemented new cost cutting measures for debt management

RALPH JONES Pg. 2

Education

MBA, Duke UniversityDurham, N.C.
B.S. University of Tennessee Knoxville, Tenn.

Affiliations

United Way of MemphisBoard of Directors
American Cancer Society Board of Directors

LOUIS ALVAREZ

1546 Elm St.   Home: 841-234-5678
Ridgewood, FL. 34589   lgs4@verizon.net   Cell: 813.313.4273

Senior Operations Manager

EXECUTIVE PROFILE

Passionate leader with diverse background in lending, collections and call center operations. Performance driven manager recognized as a cross functional team builder as well as a strong promoter of staff development for creating and executing outstanding customer service. Led acquisitions and due diligence as well as the opening, consolidating and closing down of multi unit branch operations in the southeast. Extremely passionate in implementing "outrageous customer service" theme of operations.

CORE COMPETENCIES

Auto & Mortgage Lending	Human Resources	Call Center
Customer & Vendor Mgmt.	Prime & Sub-Prime	Training/ Development
P&L Management	Multi Unit	Process Improvements

ACCOMPLISHMENTS

- Increased receivable growth by over 20% for new multi-unit branch operation, with all branches placing in top 20% in the company
- Reduced sub-prime mortgage delinquency by 5% in under 180 days
- Reduced automobile receivables delinquency by 5% in 60 days while managing portfolio of $115,000,000
- Was in the top 20% of the company in 2006 with 32% profit margin
- Reduced employee turnover by 25% utilizing self developed training system's, recognition programs and the redesign of hiring processes which increased productivity by 35% leading to over 5% reduction in delinquency
- Led company in revenue production of $1,000,000 for 7 consecutive months along with maintaining the lowest expense ratio
- Increased vendor database by 73% in less than one year
- Responsible for providing 5000 real estate appraisals monthly exceeding company standards on turn-around times by 10% and national average by 34%

ACCOMPLISHMENTS (CON'T)
- Directed 15 branch multi-unit full service lending operation
- Assisted in creating new ACD monitoring reports improving customer service levels and reducing delinquency by over 5%
- Led 2 teams with over 350 FTE and contracted employees
- Consistently produced over 25% loan volume with delinquency below company standards (5%)

PROFESSIONAL EXPERIENCE

ABC Finance	**VP Collections**	2005-2009
Walpole Finance	**Area Manager**	2001-2005
Cranapple Lending	**District Manager**	1998-2001

EDUCATION

BS in Business Management, Rollins College, Winter Park, FL.

PROFESSIONAL/SOCIAL AFFILIATIONS/CERTIFICATIONS

United Way of Florida	Big Brothers	American Heart Association

Paul Reinhold

11654 Tropicana Blvd. 941-456-7788
Clearwater, FL. 33567 pcr@verizon.net

OPERATIONS EXECUTIVE

QUALIFICATIONS SUMMARY

- Over 20 years experience in budgeting, P&L, strategic planning, compliance, marketing programs, revenue generation, expense control & reduction, repossessions and foreclosure remarketing and maintenance (REO).
- Knowledgeable in all lending, credit and collections/risk management/loss mitigation portfolios to include automobile, commercial, credit card, mortgage, small recreational vehicle and retail.
- Experienced in opening and leading call center and multi-branch lending operations with a mentality of building to exceed growth projections and cross selling all ancillary products.
- Skilled with receivables exceeding $115,000,000, as well as (multi-state) regional operations.
- Recognized for training, mentoring & developing supervisors & teams that focus on outstanding customer service.
- Outstanding communicator with great interaction and conflict management skills leading to win-win resolution results. Able to interact with all levels of management and staff.
- Supervisory level to 400+ full time and contracted employees utilizing outstanding employee retention skills.
- Proficient in developing training and marketing programs as well as procedures manuals.

Vice President Servicing Gateway Finance
Clearwater, FL 2006-2008

- Reduced delinquency by 5% by implementing customer-focused soft skills collection methods
- Decreased employee turnover by 25% by developing new hiring procedures & training programs

- Improved employee morale by creating an Employee Relations Committee (ERC)
- Developed new staff monitoring reports improving production by 30%
- Created staff trainer position to implement new 4 day training system for new hires improving retention rate

Area Manager Emerson Lending
Tampa, FL 1995-2006
- Constantly monitored appraisal fees resulting in 34% profit margin; top 5 in company and best in region
- Provided outstanding customer service resulting in leading region with 92% customer service rating
- Received Area Manager surveys results of 100% satisfaction rating utilizing pro active response agenda
- Built largest real estate staff appraiser base in region and in top 5 within the company
- Developed and implemented training program for client new hires resulting in increased client satisfaction

Education: Bachelor's of Science Business Management
University of Florida-3.94 GPA

6.
NETWORKING

THE MOST CRUCIAL SEGMENT OF YOUR JOB SEARCH IS NETWORKING. Career search statistics state that approximately 75% of jobs are found due to networking. This is commonly known as the hidden job market. Most professional jobs are not advertised and sometimes not even created until the right candidate comes along. You heard the old saying about it's who you know? Well, when it comes to career search, the saying is "It's who knows you." Wikipedia states that "**Six degrees of separation** refers to the idea that, if a person is one "step" away from each person he or she knows and two "steps" away from each person who is known by one of the people he or she knows, then everyone is no more than six "steps" away from each person on Earth." This plays into career search networking in that the assumption is you could be linked to anyone in your desired job search by six degrees, or six networking acquaintances. Some theorize that you could be connected to <u>anyone</u> by six people. For example, it is possible to be connected to the President of the United States by connecting six people. Kevin Bacon, the actor, actually created a website known as SixDegrees.org to bring charitable foundations to help the needy.

Of course, there is no map to indicate which six people you need to meet that will bring you to the CEO of the organization you wish to work for but using the concept of networking you are on the right track.

Do not get confused over networking. It is not about going around or calling everyone asking for a job. It is a mutual pact where you need to offer help to other people and hopefully in turn they will assist you. Make sure you show a sincere, bona fide interest in your daily contacts. If you attempt to fake it, they will pick up on it and not offer you any assistance. Build strong rapport with the contact and honestly keep your eyes and ears open for possibilities for them. Perhaps if they find a good job, they may be the source for you to get into that same organization and even work for this person. You will also find some joy from it once you offer a solid lead and they land the job based on this. It will most likely develop some confidence in you as well. Networking is all about building relationships.

There is no deep dark secret of what works the best. It all relates to this building of relationships. You have to continually work at it and develop a strong base of contacts. Let's say you start by meeting twelve new people and ask them each for twelve names and so on and so on. This will eventually create the six degrees for your search. But keep in mind that networking is not just to meet people, but to learn who the real decision makers are in your target organization. Obviously, networking is a numbers game and the more people you meet, the closer you are to your goal. Networking is a like a key to the door that unlocks professional relationships. It will increase your job contacts and help you to build a large database. Always make it a point to network, no matter if you are speaking to a senior executive or the clerk at the checkout where you purchase you groceries.

Too often I have met people who secured their job by a chance meeting of a center of influence. You may be speaking to the cashier at your local supermarket and her husband might just be the president of XYZ Corporation, the company at the top of your target list. I have met teachers whose spouse is a key figure at a local company, fellow church parishioners who are connected to major corporations and golf partners that have wives as HR executives. Do not miss out on any opportunities that may arise without warning. And keep in mind that your networking should not stop once you land a position. Statistics indicate your next position may not be your last and continuing to network only further develops your database of contacts. Make it a lifelong goal to network daily wherever your travels bring you. Once you become employed, it is more likely you will come in contact with the decision makers, whether within your own organization or your vendors or even competitors, so keep relationship building high on your priority list. And don't just look for the decision makers, as everyone you meet is a networking source. In fact, whether employed or not, set networking goals. Continue to monitor this goal and track your success. Most people want to help you but of course they do not want to be used just for your gain. Reciprocate as often as possible. During my search days I kept a list of my networking contacts and tracked positions that may interest them. I would refer to it continuously and forward any leads to them. It was quite satisfying to see someone land due to a lead I provided them. Everyone you meet is a good networking source for yourself as well as your other networking buddies. Just always think that everyone can help you and that you can help everyone. Your cooperation will not go unnoticed.

Your networking team is huge already keeping in mind the following list of potential networking sources:

Clergy	Relatives	Family
Neighbors	Co-workers	Vendors
Physicians	Mailman	Attorney
Mechanic	Gym/Spa	Pharmacist
Banker	Youth Orgs.	YMCA
Insurance Agent	Golf Partner	Alumni
Charities	Volunteering	Cultural
Fundraisers	Trade Shows	Address Book
Coffee Shop	Sports Events	Political Groups

The list just goes on and on, so take a brief moment and start your networking list now. Once you get going you will be surprised at how many different sources you actually have. Constantly keep it growing. One thing you want to keep in mind during your networking is that you want to look for people with influence or know those that can influence. You can often find these people standing in groups of more than two. Also, boards of local non-profit organizations and those active in community affairs will provide great opportunities. This will also direct you to becoming more involved in the community and charitable events. Keep in mind that the people you meet through these sources understand what you are going through. Many of them have been there themselves. They will be willing to help you.

Networking is not a born talent, no matter how much you may think. It is a talent that you constantly develop with no special training other than practical experience. Every time you have the opportunity, introduce yourself to someone new. During your meeting, learn whatever you can about them. Remember, people like to talk about themselves, so what an opportunity to work on building your database. The more you talk and learn, the greater your odds of making the Six Degrees of Separation work for you. But do not appear to be too aggressive in your meeting. I must stress that if you come across as you only care about yourself, they will be less likely to want to help you. Obviously, you want to promote yourself but you can do this without being overly aggressive. I have met individuals who think you should only concentrate on contacts within your field of expertise. I strongly disagree with this approach. As stated previously, you never know how that contact can help you or what acquaintances they have that will work well for you. Make all your contacts count but I list a caveat here…at networking events you need some quantity as well as quality, so don't spend the entire event with just one person. The person standing next to you in another group might prove to be a valid source as well.

Spread yourself around and make yourself well known to several potential sources. It is a good goal to set to meet 3-4 new people per networking event, obviously depending on the allowable time. In some cases you may easily have time to double those numbers. When you walk up to someone at a networking event don't ask them "so what do you do"? This appears rude to the recipient and they may not make any effort to connect with you. Work yourself into a good conversation and show interest in what they have to say. Don't spend your time with those people that you know from other networking events. Look to increase your database and meet someone new. They may even offer you new network sources that they have encountered. As I stated previously, if you make it like it is all about you, then you will receive little assistance.

We have mentioned databases previously in this chapter so let's talk a little about that before we go on. As you meet contacts, get their business card and keep a folder or loose-leaf binder where you can accumulate these cards. On each card, list something about that person that will bring them to mind for you. It might be something about their personal interests or someone you both know. It might be just where they went to college. You want to have some kind of reference should you have further conversations with them. Just think how impressed they will be when you have a conversation with them later and you congratulate them on their alma mater winning the national championship. Or, it is amazing how people react when you contact them four months later and ask them how their child did in the baseball tournament they mentioned at your first meeting.

As mentioned earlier, networking is not a talent you are born with. You must continually work at it. There are books you can read on networking that will give you some good suggestions on promoting yourself. Listed below are just a couple of books that are available at your local library.

"Power Networking" by Sandy Vilas and Donna Fisher
"Make Your Contacts Count" by A. Baber & L. Waymon.

When you attend these networking events, have an action plan before you walk in the door. Know who you want to meet and what you want to ask them. As you arrive, take a deep breath, then tell yourself you are going to meet the networking contact that will get you that dream position. Walk in tall and confident and that will carry over as you meet people there. It may be a good idea to stop in the rest room just prior, adjusting your clothes and putting that last strand of hair in place. It will only add to your self confidence in the meeting room. As you meet your contacts, shake their hand, make eye contact and smile. I once heard about a farmer who stated he would not trust anyone who would not look him in the eye. Imagine that your contact is that farmer as you shake their hand.

As far as the handshake goes, do not be a limp dish rag or Mr. Universe. The person who grabs your hand will not forget how you shake their hand. As you grab their hand, tilt yours slightly so that the area between your thumb and finger meet the same spot on their hand. It will interlock to some degree. Once you get their name, repeat it again to make sure not only that you pronounce it correctly but that it sits comfortably in your mind. If the name has a tricky pronunciation, then when you have the opportunity, jot down on the back of their business card something that will help you to pronounce it later. Of course, make sure they get one of your ample supply of business cards. This just helps in making you known to them as well. Isn't that the goal of these events? When you present your business card, there is also a proper way. As you pass the card to the recipient, hold the card with your thumb on the bottom and the next two fingers on the top held at chest high. This forces the recipient to look at your name.

    Another crucial tool for networking events is a name tag. This will help to identify you and keep your name in full view during your discussion. Make sure the letters are large enough for them to read. It may be a good idea to have your field of expertise listed as well such as Call Center Executive or Financial Analyst. That way they can associate you with your chosen field. How many times have you gone to events and you receive one of those sticky name tags that fall off as soon as you make a turn? Spend the few cents on having a professional looking name tag. You can purchase a package of six or eight along with the clear view plastic to hold them for under ten dollars. Get a couple of your networking associates to share the cost with you. You will be surprised how few people go to this extent, so you have a further opportunity to stand out from the rest. These are also great for attending job fairs as well. It makes you look professional and gives the appearance you have your "stuff together". The name tag should be on your right side so when someone shakes your hand they do not have to look in the other direction at your name tag. As you shake with your right hand their glance will automatically go to the name tag with ease. Of course the letters should be done on a computer and not hand written so as to make it look professional and obviously legible. Wearing this name tag will also make you feel more a part of the event.

    Let's discuss what you need to say during your networking events. It is most often called an elevator speech or bio. It is a self introduction lasting no more than thirty to sixty seconds. When the person walks away from you they should have an excellent idea of who you are and what you want to do. It should not be overwhelming nor be a bragging session. I remember one networking associate I had where no matter how large or how small the group or what discussion was taking place, he would make the conversation about himself. As I continued to see him at events, I noticed that the group he was in would start to shrink. It became obvious that his overbearing control of the conversation took its effect on everyone. Nothing turns someone off more than standing there listening to someone who thinks they have saved the world. Now of course, you want to have a soft pitch about some of your accomplishments but this can be accomplished in one or two sentences. Following is an example of a sixty second elevator speech. It is called an elevator speech because sixty seconds is about all the time you would have to present yourself to a networking opportunity if you were riding the elevator with that person. And remember, it is used at all networking possibilities not just on an elevator.

Elevator speeches are a necessary segment of your transitioning process. You never know where you will be and find someone asking you "So, tell me about yourself." Sound familiar? You probably had this happen not only at the interviews you have been through over the years but just in everyday meetings, even while you were employed. Develop your elevator speech and practice it over and over until you feel you have it down to a science. Practice it often in front of friends, relatives, or your significant other. If you have a tape recorder, take time to tape your speech and play it back and see where you can improve. Even better, if you have a video camera, use that. That works better because you can see your hand and body actions, and there may be areas where you can improve on that as well. Once, I taped myself, I used to play it in the auto and it would enable me to listen as if I was in the audience. It provided me with the opportunity to fine tune it.

Sample elevator speech:

"My name is John Doe and I am an operations professional with over twenty years experience in the call center industry. Most recently I served as Senior Vice President of XYZ Corporation where I increased revenue by 25% at the same time reducing expenses by 12%. I have a passion for promoting outstanding teams and have been recognized for my commitment to pursuit of outstanding customer service. I am seeking a position as Vice President or Director of a large call center in any industry. I would appreciate any leads you could offer me. Again, my name is John Doe."

This introduction tells the party your name and your profession. It touches on what you have accomplished and what you can offer an organization. In addition, it gives the individual an idea of where you are going. You can use this at any networking event, job fair, weekend social mixer, etc. Don't forget to give them your business card once you have finished with the introduction and get theirs as well. You will want to follow up with them either by phone or email. A short thank you by email will work wonders and help them not to forget you. One thing you can add to the introduction is called a "hook"; something that will make sure the networking partner will remember about you. I used to say "I provide my customers with outrageous customer service". See how that one phrase grabs your attention. You want to showcase anything unique about yourself. Show the person what benefit you can provide to an organization.

During these opportunities at networking events, look for an opportunity to invite the person to have a coffee or lunch with you. It is preferable to have coffee versus lunch due to the cost but if this contact can provide you with some excellent direction or contacts, then by all means have lunch. For example, if they are the Director of Recruiting for one of your target companies, what a great time to make a solid impression. Go for the lunch. If they accept, make sure you prepare for it and use your time efficiently. You are not there to discuss the game between the

Red Sox and Yankees. When you do have the meeting this is an excellent opportunity to present your marketing plan.

Job fairs excite some people and they feel they will leave there with a job. This is fine for the entry level positions but not at the mid-management or executive level. The company will have someone present but it may be just a low level recruiter. It is the organizations attempt to fill their entry level positions. However, it is a good place to get to the next level of gate keepers. Speak to the recruiter present and get a resume into the company but ask them for an email address of the recruiter who would be reviewing your resume. Try to get a phone number as well. This will give you an opportunity to make contact with someone who can provide you with some direction or who will know what mid to senior level positions exist that may not even be advertised yet. Ladies, make sure that when you attend these job fairs that you carry minimal items. Don't have flashy purses dangling from your shoulder. If you own a purse that you would carry with you on a Saturday night then save it for Saturday. This is not a time to have the recruiter become distracted in any way. Normally at a networking event you would not offer resumes but this is an appropriate time to offer it. Even though the recruiter present may not be aware of what is transpiring at your level they most likely will forward it to the person who does have the answers.

Here are a few pointers to keep in mind when you attend any networking events. First, be a good listener. People like to talk about themselves so give them that opportunity. Certainly you do not want them to monopolize the conversation and if you see that happening move on to the next person. But if you give them a fair chance to chat about themselves they are more likely to listen to what you have to say. It would not be common sense to interrupt them in their conversations nor polite to criticize their comments. If you do, they will not forget who you are but I guarantee they will not offer you any assistance either. This is not an appropriate time to be complaining about your career search as well. The impression left will be that of a negative person. This should be avoided at all costs.

Look for a way to direct the conversation to your goals or desires and why you are at this networking event. At these events be diversified and don't just work those who are in your industry. You don't know if you will make a contact with someone who is in technology, but as you speak to them you find out their spouse is the Human Resource Director for one of your target companies. Wouldn't this be a great opportunity to get your foot in the door? You want everyone out there promoting you. Obviously you also want to speak to those in your industry with the very least of finding out what is going on in your circle.

Arrive early at these events to take every opportunity to network. If you get there shortly after the doors open you will be able to "scope" out all the other visitors and even have quiet time to speak with them before the room fills up. And remember, you are not there to just hand out your business cards; you want to make connections. This is not a contest of who can collect the most business cards either. Going to a two hour event and coming away with 32 business cards is not productive. Most likely you will not even remember most of the people you met anyway, as you were on a whirlwind tour. Make sure that any business cards you do collect you pronounce their name before walking away. This will give the impression that you are truly interested in knowing and remembering them. When you receive a business card, your looking at it immediately will show the individual you care about receiving their card. Once you walk away jot something on the card to help you remember who they were. It may be something about what you talked about, such as their hobby or family. List the event on it so you will have an easier time remembering what they looked like. Put the business card in a pocket separate from where you keep your own personal cards. You do not want to accidentally give out a card you received thinking it was your own.

Let's discuss how to work a room when you arrive. If you walk in and there is a group already formed discussing something, first look to see how many in the group. If it is a group of ten people, avoid it. It will be difficult to break in and be noticed in a positive way. On the other hand if there is a wall flower standing all by themselves, avoid them as well. They most likely will not be overly helpful. Ideally you want to be able to break into a group of two or three. Your presence will be felt and you will have more opportunity to enter their conversation. If the group is struggling for conversation, do your part. Anyone can make small talk. You don't want to walk into the group and start asking everyone what their occupation is either.

The old standby of discussing weather is a good start but be creative about it. If you walk up and say "Is it supposed to rain today?" that may not prove too exciting. Try something like "Did you hear that the weatherman has predicted another depression in the Tropics?" This will most likely create more interest and enthusiasm. Ask about market trends, travel plans or hobbies. Discuss where they went to college. Everyone likes to brag about their alma mater. Family or where they are originally from will open the door to increased conversation. These are personal topics and usually close to their hearts. You can intelligently direct the conversation your way eventually. Ask them what their interests are or what challenges they faced at their last job. Pretend you are interviewing them and that should really create some conversation for you. The conversation will eventually get to what your profession is and what you are looking for and as it does, make sure it is not all about you.

Offer some assistance to them. Perhaps you know some leads or contacts that you can parlay to your advantage. They will be more likely to help you when the time comes if they know you are generally interested in them as well. There may be others at the event that you know could prove to be valuable to these contacts…introduce them to each other. And don't be afraid to ask for help. Most people enjoy helping out and will offer some great leads.

As you work the room, create a plan of attack by identifying those who may prove the most beneficial to you. You want to make each and every minute count. This does not mean that if someone approaches you and his or her profession is of no interest to you, don't just walk away. Be polite and give them ample time to present their case. As stated previously, you don't know who their contacts are. But if you see the conversation dragging on and all they want to do is talk about the weather, move on. These events are not for sitting there with your friends discussing last night's game but for networking. Meet people who you do not know. When you enter the room, feel like you belong there. I remember one associate of mine that stopped at the door just before he went in and said to himself "Charge" and continued on into the event. He felt it gave him that little bit of extra confidence. And by all means, smile throughout the event. Another tip is to make sure you meet the speaker. Too often the audience is afraid to go up to the speaker and meet them so your path to them should be wide open. Let the speaker know you were impressed with their presentation. This speaker may be so pleased that you made the attempt to meet them that they may offer you some job search tips, including other referral sources.

Once you leave the networking event, make sure you do something with the business cards you collected. Send them an email thanking them for their time. This will show them you did not forget them and that you were interested in what they had to say. You never know if this contact is the one who will get you by the gatekeeper. How often you keep in contact depends on how good the contact was. The one whose spouse was the HR Director of your target company should be contacted often. This does not mean daily but it would not hurt to email them once a week. If they feel it is too often they will let you know. Offer to have coffee with them and meet with them to continue any discussions you had and trade job leads at the same time.

Scheduling these events require good planning. Your calendar should be no less than two weeks out and preferably three to four weeks. Of course you will share this calendar with your family and management team. They may be able to offer you suggestions on how to fill up that white space. You want to have something going on constantly. Keep in mind that looking for a new position is a job in itself. Much of the white space can be filled with recurring events such as weekly networking events, Chamber of Commerce meetings, career counselor meetings, financial planning, etc. Look for adding new meetings or job fairs. Watch the business section of your local newspaper for upcoming events. Many times they will have a calendar with the following week's events.

Where can I network? Such a common question with so many, many obvious answers. Do you belong to any church groups, civic organizations or do you coach your child's soccer team? Are there local volunteer organizations such as Lions Club, Rotary, Kiwanis or others? If you are a member of one of these organizations look to get on the board of directors. Perhaps there is a local cause that is important to you and lobby to become a board of director. Not only will you be building some good contacts as these are the business people in your community, but you will be giving your time for a cause you truly believe in and this will come across to others in the same group. In addition, this will serve as a good stress reliever. Volunteering for Habitat for Humanity creates some great contacts. Do you have a local Toastmasters organization? How about your college placement center? Once you graduate that does not have to be the end of it. Any college will continue to offer you placement services. Take advantage of it.

How about each of your neighbors, family, friends, postman, hairdresser or barber, pharmacist, doctor, lawyer, adult sports leagues, cultural associations, banker, mechanic and homeowners associations. The list goes on and on and I am sure you could add many more to this. Are there any trade shows or lectures that you could attend to build some contacts? Watch newspapers for executives that have been recently promoted and send them a congratulations card along with your business card. They just may follow up with you to find out who you are. Remember your business card may not have your profession on it and they could be curious, especially if they are in any form of marketing position. They are constantly looking for leads and obviously by their recent promotion they are go-getters.

Look for people strongly connected to the community, as they will know many people. Sit down and develop a list of 50-75 people that you would like to get to know and start a plan to meet them. Many newspapers will have a calendar of upcoming events that you can work into your schedule. It might just be a meeting of others with the same hobby. The majority of these meetings is held at night and will not interfere with your job search during the day. And this will provide you with an excuse to socialize at a minimal cost. Furthermore, many times these meetings are visited by the senior executives that are unable to get away from their job during the workday. They will usually be more relaxed and open to conversation, not always looking at their watch.

    Can you teach a course at a local college? This will put you in contact with a wide variety of people. Do not be naïve to think only young adults take these courses. Many times executives want to brush up on certain skills associated with their profession such as Excel or PowerPoint. I once took a course on photography that was being taught by someone who was knowledgeable in photography as they had their own studio, which was built on providing wedding photographs. They eventually were hired by the city council to provide photographs for a promotion of the city. How many business men and woman do you think he knew? Perhaps you can even create your own networking group. I attended one group with individuals that attended other networking meetings throughout the week. This group met in a coffee shop and not only discussed what was going on in our searches but each person usually provided events that could be listed on our calendars which the rest of the group was not aware of. Let's go one step further and become part of a spiritual group at your church. These groups also usually meet in the evening and will provide some great support during this time of need.

Below is a list of some organizations with their website that may prove to be a valuable asset to you:

American Association of Healthcare Administrative Mgmt.	zaham.org
Association of Energy Engineers	aee.org
Association of IT Professionals	aitp.org
American Marketing Association	marketingsource.com
Call Center Networking Group	ccng.com

International Customer Service Association	icsa.com
Institute of Electrical and Electronic Engineers	ieee.org
International Management Accountants	imanet.org
Institute of Supply Management	ism.ws
National Association of Credit Managers	nacm.org
Project Management Institute	pmi.org
Society of Human Resources Management	shrm.org
Society of Manufacturing Engineers	sme.org

Some other leads may be researching your profession at the local library or business trend magazines. Many cities have newspapers that are weekly and devote the issue to business happenings in the area. For example, in Florida there is the Tampa and Jacksonville Business Journal. Orlando and Miami also offer it as well. The publisher of this newspaper also publishes this in many cities throughout the country. Check your library out for employment recruiter's guides that will break them down by the professions they represent such as accounting, credit, financial, lending, manufacturing, or technology. Also purchase either a copy of the Wall Street Journal or New York Times newspapers as they offer what is going on around the United States as well as global.

Let's summarize what this chapter has taught us. First, get out and be seen. You will not find a job sitting at your desk playing video games or surfing the Internet. Although the Internet is a viable source, it is neither the only source nor the most important one. Do not rely on your friends to find you a job. They have their own issues and you are not their top priority. Use them but do not abuse them. Use all the contacts you develop to set up meetings if only for coffee. At these coffee meetings do not give out your resume and at best offer your marketing plan. Follow up all events and meetings with thank you emails and follow up with them often. Keep in mind you are attending these events to assist in advancing your search as well as those others you meet. Make sure you show up with a war plan. Know what you want to accomplish, whom you want to see, and what you want to say. This means have your elevator speech ready to go. Practice it before you leave home. As the old American Express commercial goes; "Don't leave home without it." And also keep in mind that you are not trying to win a contest for collecting the most business cards, but making quality connections. Show interest in your party by keeping eye contact; get their business card and smile.

There are several online networking sources that can prove beneficial. The largest is Linkedin.com. As of the writing of this book, there were over 40 million users of Linkedin throughout the world. Its basic concept is akin to the Six degrees of separation theory. This is a free service, if you use the basic model. Once you sign up, look for those that you have worked with in the past and send them an invitation. Once they accept the invitation, you now have access to their network. At the time of this writing, I had approximately 200 contacts that provided me with just over 5 million potential contacts. You can join different groups on Linkedin. There are groups for banking executives, IT professionals, call centers, Christian organizations, etc. It would be insane not to take advantage of a free service that provides you the possibility to link up with people all over the world. Sign on today and build your profile and get those contacts invited.

Go to http://learn.Linkedin.com/training/ to learn how to use Linkedin properly. It will teach you everything from how to join to creating a group.

"At the end of the day, you bet on people not strategies."
-Larry Bossidy

7.
USING THE INTERNET & RECRUITERS

THE INTERNET SERVES A GOOD PURPOSE AND SHOULD NOT BE avoided. Most career counselors will tell you that few positions are obtained through the Internet and that is true. As we previously mentioned in the Networking chapter, approximately 75% of all positions obtained come about due to networking. However, it is imperative you cover all the bases. Use each and every source that is available to you and the Internet is readily available. Of course spending twenty hours per week searching the Internet is wasting valuable time that can be used elsewhere to produce stronger results. The key to a good career search is balance, but that does not mean you spend 10 hours networking, 10 hours on the Internet, etc. It means that you need to get the word out regarding your job search as quick and as often as possible. The Internet will help serve this purpose. Several times I have obtained positions through the Internet but on the other hand I have also obtained positions through networking. If networking provides 75% of the career positions out there, then what would you think is an appropriate amount of time to spend networking?

Many job search sites such as Monster and CareerBuilder offer you the opportunity to post your resume on their site. Recruiters will search these sites looking for appropriate candidates. The cost is free and it takes little time to post your resume. These sites actually track how often your resume is viewed by recruiters and employers so you can monitor the results of your postings. They also give you the opportunity to post up to five resumes, so you can have several versions available with each geared to the type of position you are seeking. Only one can be active but it is quite easy to change this setting should you see a position that better meets your preferences. For example, you may qualify for a CFO positions or for a Controller position, so have a resume for each position. If you see a CFO position and the Controller resume is the active one, then just change the setting to make the CFO resume active. By having a resume for each position, you will have to make fewer corrections or changes when you see a particular position. I do want to stress here that never fabricate any of your expertise or knowledge. It always has a way of coming back to haunt you. Keep your integrity foremost in your thoughts and work.

There are many job sites available, some catering to certain occupations. Bankjobs.com lends itself to the banking industry while Indeed.com and Direct Employers.com allows you to enter the type of position you are seeking along with an occupational area and it will pull up those positions from all of the active Internet sites. The industry will make very little difference. Some sites cater to the executive level position such as 6figurejobs.com, which lists positions with salary's exceeding $100,000 in salary. There are other sites such as Callcentercareers.com and Callcenterops.com that cater to the call center industry. Most companies have websites with career sections as a link such as Home Depot, HSBC, and Bank of America to name just a few. One great recruiting source is Management Recruiters International, a firm that has a site that covers the entire United States. You can enter more than one area of expertise as well as a geographical area and it will search each of these parameters. Ladders.com is another executive site that provides positions with salaries above $100,000; however this is not a free site. There is a monthly fee to use it and depending on your career choices, it may or may not be feasible to join. You can cancel at any time so there are no long-term contracts.

Again, I want to caution you that only small portions of jobs are listed on the Internet. You may pull up a geographical area and see hundreds listed but many are entry-level positions. Mid to senior level management positions are few and far between. Most sites allow you to enter at least one geographical area. This is especially good if you are looking to relocate to another area where you have not built up any networking contacts, nor is it convenient to network due to the distance. At the very least, the site will list positions that may not apply to you but will provide company websites to permit you to contact the company direct for other positions that may provide a good fit for your qualifications. For example, you may live in Phoenix and wish to relocate to Boston but you are not sure what companies exist there. Searching the Internet for Boston will list the positions in the area you designate, such as accounting, manufacturing, or operations. There may be a position for an IT person at XYZ Company and you are in accounting. You will now know that XYZ Company is located in Boston and you can go directly to their website for all available jobs.

The Internet is an excellent source to research a company. Let's say you live in Chicago and you are interviewing with a company based out of Orlando. You may not know anything about the company so go to the Internet and enter the company name. The company will most likely have quite a lot to offer on the website. Some areas that will be listed are contact information, history of the company, what they do, other positions that are available, and even their annual financial reports. Some sites list recent media announcements, so this will give you a good idea of new products or services that the company is offering.

Another method you can use is Google alerts. With this, you are able to list certain key words or company names and save them in the system. Whenever something hits the Internet with these key words you are sent an alert. Let's say that you want to have an alert that picks up any key words regarding pharmaceuticals. Each time something in the pharmaceutical field hits the Internet, you will get an email. The caution here is that some areas, such as pharmaceuticals, may cause you to be bombarded with emails regarding pharmaceutical products, so be specific about what you list. For example if you are in the banking industry and you are interested in a position in product knowledge for credit cards, each time a company puts an ad on the Internet for low credit card rates, you will get hits. It is your decision if it is worth the extra trouble. You can do the same thing with a company. If you want to know every time XYZ Company posts something or someone else posts something about XYZ Company, you will also get an alert. One good thing here is that if there are negative reports about XYZ Company you will know firsthand about it, as the company site may not list anything negative.

Some of these job-posting sites even offer other services such as resume writing. Once you post your resume you will surely get emails advising you of this service. Keep in mind that you do not have to use this service to post your resume or perform a job search. Should you decide to use their resume writing service, it is not free. You will have to determine if the cost is necessary at this time. They may even have an area that lists job fairs. This is another free service and may prove helpful to you. Of course, by using these sites you will be the recipient of sales offers such as independent education offers, such as DeVry University and Keiser University.

Your local unemployment office most likely will have a site where you can view jobs that are available in your immediate area. In addition, it may help you seek positions in areas that you are not familiar with such as if you live in Richmond, Va. and you are seeking a position in Florida, all you have to do is go to My Florida.com and it will pull up a section on jobs in Florida. By going further into the site a map with all of the counties in Florida will show. Then just click on the county where you are seeking a position and all available positions listed with the agency will show. Again, this is a free service and you may be surprised at what you see.

Some other sites that may prove valuable are listed below:

Advisorteam.com	Collegegrad.com
HireAccounting.com	Aimmconsult.com
College911.com	Hirediversity.com
Assessment.com	Constructiononly.com
Hotjobs.com	Careerlab.com
Engineeringjobs.com	Kiersey.com

For those baby boomers, here are two other good sites:

Jobs4pointo.com   Retirementjobs.com

Let's discuss recruiters at this point. They are a viable source to assist you in getting in the door for positions that may not even be advertised. The company they represent normally pays these recruiters and you should note here their allegiance will be with that company. Their fees range from 20-40% of the first year salary of the candidate. So if the position pays salary and bonus of $100,000 annually, the recruiters fee will be anywhere from $20,000 to $40,000. The most positive benefit here is that these recruiters will know all about any positions before they are even advertised, if in fact they do even get posted. Many times they are not posted and the company will allow the recruiter to locate qualified candidates without performing any internal measures to locate a viable candidate.

What you must realize if you have never dealt with an independent recruiter before is that they represent the company. Do not expect these recruiters to call you every day with status updates nor should you hinder their progress by calling them daily. This is the biggest complaint most candidates have, in that they sit back and do not hear anything. If the recruiter has something important to relay to you they will call you. Make sure they have the appropriate contact information available to them such as any possible contact numbers for you. It will be frustrating at times when you attempt to contact them and do not hear anything back but if you are going to be using recruiters, get use to it. Perhaps they do not have anything to report to you at this time. They too have to rely on any feedback from the company and many times they do not get it. It seems that in the last five years companies are slower in making decisions. When you do attempt to contact them I would suggest you do so early morning or late in the afternoon. If you are going to reach them this is probably the best time. The rest of their day is spent on the phone locating positions. Keep in mind they also shop clients. Let's say you have strong qualifications as a VP of Inventory Control. The recruiter will contact companies that have this need thus shopping your skills. This takes time and can be a hit or miss situation. But, however you leave it with the recruiter, stay on them. By keeping in contact with them you ensure you are not "forgotten."

There are two different types of recruiters: retained and contingency. A retained recruiter is guaranteed a fee no matter what. If they get the job posting and they do not locate the eventual hire, they still get paid. Retained recruiters usually handle executive level searches where salaries easily exceed $100,000. A contingency recruiter will only receive a fee if they locate the candidate and he/she is hired. They may at times market candidates but usually after a posting is placed with their firm. Either recruiter receives their fee from the employer and not the candidate. Normally the retained recruiter will receive 1/3 of the fee when the order is placed, another 1/3 midway through the search and the balance at the end of the search.

I would strongly suggest that if you have applied to a company before you contacted the recruiter, don't pass that on to the recruiter. They may have a tendency to not try and sell you to the company, concerned they will not receive a fee. There is a possibility that if you applied for the position and then contacted the recruiter, he or she will not be considered to have supplied the candidate. But if you keep this information confidential and let the recruiter attempt to locate a position for you, the company may not be aware of your prior resume and with the recruiter representing you, the chances could be better.

Make sure you present all of your qualifications to the recruiter. Give them all possible options to showcase your talents. If you have presented all of your skills and qualifications, it will give the recruiter the opportunity to show the company how you can be an asset to them. Once you submit your resume to the recruiter the next step will be to have a personal conversation with them, either by phone or face to face. The recruiter will know how to dig into your background and bring out all of your assets. If you mail or email your resume to the recruiter, make sure your cover letter also brings out all of your attributes. It will only assist the recruiter further in his attempt to get you placed.

Remember that the recruiter is not going to send all of the candidates he has received resumes from to the company, just the best ones. He may place two or three and let the company decide which the best candidates are but he will never submit all of his candidates so this is further reason to show you are the best. These recruiters have an advantage you do not have. They know who the decision makers are and have built relationships with them. Let them use their contacts and expertise to get your resume in the door. Once the company has reviewed your resume and feels you are a viable candidate, then the rest will be up to you. Had you not had your resume forwarded to this company, they may not have ever seen it through other sources.

Your local library can provide you with some great sources of books on recruiters. There are many books that will provide names and contact information throughout the United States for recruiters in the field you desire. Many of these books will break them down by either retained or contingency or even by field of expertise. If you are looking for a manufacturing position, there are specialized recruiters for this area.

Looking for a recruiter in the banking industry? Have no fear because these books will cover this area as well. You really want to direct your efforts to recruiters that handle your occupation. Submitting your resume to a recruiter who specializes in manufacturing and you are in banking will not serve you well. I have a friend who was seeking a position in her background of credit card operations. When she approached one recruiter he was so impressed with her qualifications that he shopped her around. He finally found a financial institution that although they did not have a position available, they created one.

Whatever way you go, use this great source. As mentioned above, these recruiters have built the relationships and know the jobs that are not advertised. They also know how to sell you to a company when a position is not even available. There are hundreds of examples of recruiters "selling" someone to a company with the talents that provide a good fit and a position is created. You may not be able to do this. Of course your local telephone book also provides you with the names and phone numbers of those in your immediate area. Do not settle for just contacting one recruiter; contact three or four. It does not cost you anything and you need to be as visible to the hiring companies as much as possible.

Another form of networking is online networking such as Linkedin.com. This is a fast growing method of connecting with people around the world. It is based on the Six Degrees of Separation concept. Let's say you live in Boston and you have a close friend that lives in San Diego. Assuming you are both registered with Linkedin, you have access to each others' contacts. For example, at the time of this writing I had approximately 200 contacts which connected me to over 5 million professionals. Now, back to your friend in Boston who let's say has 150 contacts. One of those contacts works as a CIO with Bank of America. This is the company and area you wish to work in so you ask your friend to introduce you to him via the Internet. He brings you both together and now you have a high level contact, and possibly your next boss, at your target company.

Linkedin.com also has groups that you can belong to, in areas such as human resources, technology, manufacturing, banking, etc. You can join any of these groups and meet the members of that group. I have contacts in India and England. Belonging to any of these groups entitles you to carry on group discussions or even post the position you are seeking. You can also job search through Linkedin. All you have to do is insert the zip code for the area in which you are seeking. There are jobs listed that are only listed on Linkedin. Sometimes a company requests candidates who have some personal recommendations. These recommendations come from your contacts. Take advantage of this opportunity. Go to previous supervisors and ask for their recommendation. Have you worked on special projects with some employees in other departments of your company? Seek their recommendations as well. It would not even hurt to obtain recommendations from those you worked with on community involvement projects or even non-profit committees.

You can post your photo on the site as well as create a short profile of your attributes. This way someone who views your personal site can get a good glimpse of who you are. This is a free service and gives you the opportunity to be seen throughout the world. Recruiters heavily use this site to meet their needs. Don't be surprised if a recruiter contacts you after seeing your profile on this site. Another segment of the site is the Questions and Answers. Many of those listed on the site ask questions of the members. You can answer these questions and have your answers posted for all to see. Providing a top notch answer not only gets you a good rating but will show just what you are made of.

"Be the change you want to see in the world."
$$\qquad\qquad\qquad\qquad\qquad\qquad\qquad\text{-Mahatma Gandhi}$$

8.
INTERVIEWING

ALL OF THOSE LONG HOURS NETWORKING, PREPARING RESUMES, and sending them out has finally paid off. You received a call from the human resources department and they want to schedule you for an interview. First thing up is take a deep breath and as difficult as it may be, do not get too excited. This is just another step in the entire process. You must prepare for the interview as if receiving the job depends on it. Keep in mind that a positive interview is very important and you have to put an extreme amount of emphasis on the preparation. Although your resume got you to this point, remember that the hiring party will not be hiring based solely on your qualifications as indicated on your resume. The resume only gets you through the door and now the rest is up to you. Your qualifications are known as hard skills but what are truly going to get your hired are the soft skills. These soft skills are what separate the good from the best candidates. Most companies hire people they like and feel will fit into their organization, not necessarily the most qualified due to their skill set. Soft skills are the people skills and will determine if you are a good fit for the organization.

Your interviewer will be looking for certain attributes such as people skills, communication, creativity or even your decision making skills to help them finalize their decision. You may have had the best resume that was submitted but if you bomb out on the interview, then all was for nothing. What we will cover in this chapter is how to prepare as well as how you should handle yourself during the interview, whether it is a face to face or phone interview. Too many highly qualified candidates have lost out on the position due to lack of preparation for the interview. This includes everything from making sure your fingernails are manicured to reviewing the prospective company in detail. Being well prepared not only gives you an edge on the competition but increases your confidence walking into the interview. Taking five or ten minutes to prepare for it just prior to the interview will get you nothing except a quick exit.

The most prominent and widely used interview is the behavioral interview. This type of interview will give the interviewer a considerable indication of most of your current behavioral tendencies and characteristics and how you handled previous situations. How you handled these past situations will prove to be a good indicator of how you will perform in the future, if you are brought onboard. This is the general foundation for the behavioral type of interview. It is much more difficult to exaggerate the past as there is little preparation because the questions asked are not text book. The best way to handle these interviews is with the SAR method: Situation, Action and Results. Behavioral interviews will relate to accountability as well as action of your previous performances. This type of interview is used because it is more difficult to prepare for and book answers play little part here. If the interviewer is prepared for it, their questions will determine whether you are motivated and determine whether you are a team player or not. Keep all of your answers short and to the point. If you do not understand the question, do not be afraid to ask them to repeat it.

This may be the first of two or more interviews and the interviewer will be looking for reasons to eliminate you until they are down to the final two or three candidates. These behavioral interviews will reveal to the employer how you work under pressure, how you relate to other team members and are you a decisive leader. They may also indicate what type of judgment you use and whether you have integrity and honesty. Be alert to the questions they ask in a behavioral interview. For example they may ask you "Tell me about a time when you bent the rules a little." This is most probably a trick question. What they may be looking for is whether you do bend rules. If you actually give them an instance when you have bent the rules, they will assume this is normal attitude in your daily performance. Before you answer any of these behavioral questions, evaluate the question and determine what behavior it actually relates to. What scenario can you offer that best relates to what the company is looking for?

Another type of face to face interview is the functional interview which will be easier to prepare for. It does not deal so much with how you would handle past behavior as it does with questions relating to your resume and what you did at each of your past employers. It is much easier to provide programmed types of answers here and does not necessarily indicate who the best candidate is and whether they will fit in. A third type of interview is the informational interview which may be granted when a position is not even available. The hiring party, usually a senior manager, will be trying to determine whether you would be a good fit for the organization. There are many cases that a person has performed so well at an informational interview that a position was created for them. Keep in mind that you are always interviewing, whether it is in a formal interview or just speaking to someone on the elevator.

Let's start with your attire as you prepare for the interview. It would seem comedic to say that you do not ever wear shorts or t-shirts to an interview but believe me it does happen. It is bad enough that some people throw caution to the wind and dress very flamboyant. It is better to err on the side of conservatism. You have heard the old saying "dress for success" and there is no reason not to believe this is best. Make sure the shoes are polished and I did say shoes, not tennis shoes. Keep your college pins as well as any outside organizational pins at home. Your interviewer may not share your same interests or views. What if you wore your college pin and did not realize that your college just beat the alma mater of your interviewer?" Some hiring individuals may take this very personal and should you be one of two finalists and the other person happened to be an alumni of your interviewers college or high school, where do you think that would leave you? Why take a chance to find out?

Men, wear a solid color blue or black suit with a conservative tie and long sleeve white shirt. The ties should not match the shirt but blend nicely. For example, don't wear a dark blue tie with a dark blue suit. There are some thoughts that black suits are depressing but that is a matter of opinion. Don't wear the bright paisley tie your mother gave you for Christmas. Dark socks and polished shoes are important as well. Ladies, again a solid color conservative suit with a color coordinated blouse creates the professional look. White is the preferred color of a blouse as it gives a professional and authoritative look to your outfit. If your preference is a dress, make sure it is not too short. Female interviewers are not as forgiving about this fashion item as male interviewers. No brightly colored hosiery;.light colored are ideal. Keep your jewelry minimal and carry some form of briefcase if possible. If not, carry a conservative purse and not the one you would take to the beach or to the opera. Above all, make sure your clothes are neat and pressed. Once you walk in with a wrinkled shirt or blouse, the interview is basically over.

Perform a dry run of trying on the clothes you plan on wearing. Take a look in the mirror and make sure everything looks good. This will save you time and perhaps embarrassment the day of the interview. You may find something needs pressing or cleaning. Maybe there is a spot on the tie you forgot about. Are there loose threads on the clothing? As you get dressed, think about the climate. Will these clothes put you in a position of being too hot or too cold? You want to be middle of the road because you do not know what the temperature will be in the office. Perhaps the interviewer likes a cold office or just the opposite.

Make sure the haircut is neat and trimmed and certainly not like you just came in from the beach. Ladies, do not give the impression that you just walked through the cologne section of your favorite store. If your perfume is much too strong it may come across as offensive to the interviewer. Keep the cologne light, should you feel you must wear any at all. Many people can become offended by certain fragrances and their focus will be on that "awful" odor throughout the interview. Just days ago I was sitting at a meeting next to a middle aged woman who had such a strong fragrance that during a break I actually moved my seat. Your fingernails should be neat and trimmed, and one last thing about your outfit ladies, keep the make-up professional. You are not interviewing for a position at the carnival. If in doubt, leave it out. This may sound critical but many people do not have the knack for knowing what looks good on them and what does not.

It wasn't that many years ago that the discussion of tattoos and body piercing was even necessary during this topic, however it is necessary. Over the years I have interviewed many applicants who proudly wore their tattoos and body piercings in the interview and I must admit my focus was not where it should be. Remove the piercings and cover those tattoos if possible. Then we have the topic of smoking. Obviously most people are intelligent enough not to pull out the cigarette pack during the interview and light up but what about just before you walk into the building? Do you have that last smoke to calm your nerves? Don't do it. Smoke has a way of adhering itself to your clothes and the odor does not easily go away so pass on the cigarette and eat a mint instead. In fact, it is advisable to eat a mint or chew some gum before the interview to hide any odors from meals or previous cigarettes.

To complete your outfit bring along a nice, professional looking briefcase or portfolio. You will not only feel professional but you will look the part. Besides, it will give you something to take notes with. Of course, before you start writing during the interview, ask the interviewer for permission. This will show further professionalism. You need all the "points" you can accumulate.

We have covered all of the personal hygiene and attire items for preparing. Obviously before you leave your home, stand in front of the mirror for a once over. What you must do next is make sure you are prepared for the interview itself. Presentation is another major step once you walk into the interview. Remember that once you walk into the building the interview has started. Some people may say the interview starts when you pull into the parking lot. I can remember one interview that I actually walked in the front door ahead of the interviewer who I had not met previously. Fortunately I had held the door open for them rather than let it slam in their face. It is advisable to be courteous as well as polite to everyone once you enter the parking lot. You never know who the other party is.

One other situation I found myself in was as I was leaving an interview I awaited the elevator and just as I got on, the doors starting closing as a woman was trying to get on. I was able to hit the door open button to let her on. Later, after I started with the company, I found out this was the wife of president of the company. What kind of impression would it had left if I did not catch the elevator doors? The gate keeper can be almost as important as the interviewer. Introduce yourself to them and offer a business card to them and make sure you have a big smile on your face. Make sure you scan the desk for one of theirs as well. When you send the interviewer a thank you card send the gate keeper one as well, and make sure you hand write them neatly and legibly. Carry on a good conversation with them while you wait. This is an ideal time to ask some questions to get you a better picture of the company and show your interest as well. This gate keeper may be called on to state how you acted during the wait and if you give them the wrong impression, even if it is only one item, then that is all they will carry forth. Sitting in the reception area "chomping" on your fingernails when this nicely manicured receptionist is looking at you... well you get the picture. Make sure you turn your cell phone off when you enter the building. It could be embarrassing if it goes off during the interview. Let's go back to the preparation process.

Use every resource possible to learn about the company. Google the interviewers name or go to the Internet for information on the company. Many organizational websites have links that will give you information on recent press clippings. Review each of them because these are published by newspapers and other sources. These clippings will be recent and will announce anything exciting going on in the company or a charity that the company has recently supported. Who knows but that charity might be just one that you have an interest in or know the local director and that would provide you with another networking partner? It will also give you an ice-breaker to get you started in the interview itself. Find out how large the company is, what they do, who the officers are and what their favorite charities are. Become familiar with the company website because if a question comes up during the interview this website may provide you with some clues. Do your homework and learn all you can.

Now that you know everything about the company, start preparing for the interview itself. Research any possible questions that could arise during the interview and have answers ready. You do not want to recite word for word from the books you read but present them in a way that makes it sound like it was right from you.

There are hundreds of questions that could be asked so obviously you will not know them all but following are a few sample questions that could be asked.

- Tell me about yourself.
- Why are you leaving your current job?
- Why have you had so many jobs?
- Have you ever supervised other employees?
- What are your strengths?
- What are your weaknesses?
- What was your biggest disappointment in your career?
- Can you multi-task?
- Will you relocate now or if a promotion were offered to you?
- What do you know about this position?
- Do you get bored easily?
- Tell me about a conflict you had with a supervisor or subordinate?
- Describe a time when you were dissatisfied with your performance.
- How do you stay current with changes in your field of expertise?
- Why should I hire you rather than someone internally?
- What interests you least about this position?
- How do you handle rejection?
- What areas do you feel you need to improve on?
- How would your coworkers describe you?
- How would your subordinates describe you?
- What would you do differently in your career?
- Describe a "poor supervisor" that you had.
- Discuss the worst boss you ever had.

- Are you able to travel frequently for work?

Many state agencies are offering virtual interviews. You sit in front of a monitor and a programmed presentation appears. You will actually receive relevant questions from the interviewer, already pre-programmed depending on your profession. They will ask you questions and your answer will be taped for your review and a critique at the end of the presentation. It is amazing the habits we bring to an interview and are not even aware of it. Contact your local unemployment office to see if they offer this. You can always practice at home if you have a camcorder. Have your spouse or a member of your management team ask you some questions that they have prepared. Preparing them yourself does not present any element of surprise and it will be a little more difficult to have "pat" answers when you do not know the question. Have your interviewer grill you hard. It is less costly to make a mistake here versus the actual interview. The harder the questions, the more you will be prepared for the actual interview.

Give yourself plenty of time to prepare for the interview. When you are called to set up the interview, schedule it according to your schedule, allowing some flexibility. Usually the caller will have a couple of available times and you have the option to select one. If you are not a morning person then schedule it for the afternoon. Allow yourself enough time for the interview. If you have a medical appointment at 2 p.m. don't schedule the interview for 1 p.m. Do not forget about travel time. The traffic may be fine at 2 p.m. but hectic at 9 a.m. Allow sufficient time to get there. It is advisable to make a dry run to the location prior to the interview. The dry run should happen at the same time (on a previous day) as the interview. This will give you some idea of the traffic at that time of the day. Having an interview at 9 a.m. and doing a practice run at 2 p.m. will not give you a good picture of travel time. The dry run will also give you a solid travel plan on getting there. Perhaps you are not familiar with that area of the city and a practice run will change that. When you speak to the caller in setting up the interview, get the exact details of where to go. I have heard many stories of someone going to the wrong company location for the interview. Learn the correct building, what floor the interview is on and who to see when you get there. Many companies have campuses where there are four or five buildings and the distance between each is large due to individual parking lots. The caller may not be the one who you will report to.

Prior to your interview you need to spend time researching the company. Remember that not only does the company want someone that provides a good fit, but you need to make sure that the company will provide a good fit for your career. Research the web to find out as much as you can about the company. Keep in mind that the web is open 24/7 so getting access should not be a problem. If you do not know their web address, you can call the company's main telephone and obtain that information. Or you can Google their name and odds are that it will most definitely show up. Now, after spending time on the web searching and nothing turns up, this is reason to be cautious about the company. Is it their intent to remain unknown or overly discreet and if so, why? If you have the opportunity, obtain a copy of the last annual financial statement. Many times this can be found right on their website. Is the company experiencing growth or has there been a down turn?

When you do receive the phone call from a recruiter to set up the interview ask if there is some scheduling flexibility for the appointment and then schedule it for early am or late pm and not the middle of the day. The interviewer will be more likely to remember who you are if you are one of the first in the morning or last in the afternoon. There is the chance that if you are coming in the middle of the day and you are one of many, then you may not stand out. Of course, if there is no flexibility in scheduling, which is rare, then take what you can get. You can always offset this by good interview preparation. If you are able to, get a copy of the job description and build the practice interview around these questions. You know the old saying about practice makes perfect. It also may be advisable to ask what days are available for an interview and schedule it to be one of the first or one of the last. More chance of being remembered. I prefer to go last as you will most likely be on that persons mind all weekend.

What you want to bring to an interview is the following:

- A professional looking portfolio
- Any letters of recommendation you have, professional and personal
- Copies of previous awards that you have won
- Copies of your resume, preferably in some form of binder such as what you used to put your school essays and book reports in. Make sure the paper is of good quality.

Alright, the day has come and you have arrived in the parking lot. Take a deep breath and clear out the cobwebs. Just look at it like you are meeting a new friend. All of your hard work at networking and preparing your resume has worked..you got the interview. Make sure you arrive early even if you have to wait in the lobby for awhile. You have already practiced the drive there so you should have allowed for plenty of time. When you enter the building, take a look around and get a feel for the culture before you speak to anyone. If there is a rest room available take a minute and visit it making any last adjustments to your clothing. Pay attention to the little things. If there is a receptionist, introduce yourself and let her know who you are there to see and make sure you smile. Remember the interview started once you walked through the door. Make pleasant conversation with her as you wait. Do make sure you cell phone is off, not just on vibrate. It will be discerning if it should ring or vibrate during the interview and you stand the chance of being thrown off your game a little. One big mistake I have seen many times is bringing others with you, to include children, spouses or friends. This is your interview and you need to be focused on the task at hand. Leave them home or at a daycare center.

While you are sitting there in the reception area be at your best. You do not know who is watching you and at the very least the receptionist will be. Be under the impression that this gatekeeper is the hiring party. Obviously they are not but they may have the ear of the hiring party. Do what you can to engage them in conversation. It will help you to learn about the organization as well as let them know about your personality and whether it will be a good fit. I do remember walking into an organization once and it turned out that the Director of HR just happened to be filling in for the receptionist while she went to lunch, which I did not know. Without a doubt she was watching every move I made. If there are magazines relating to the company or your field of expertise, read them. You may find an article in one of these magazines that could relate to your target company.

Now it is time to take the next step. The receptionist is directing you to the hiring party or recruiter for your interview. Take a deep breath and relax. As you walk into their office take a glance around the room noticing something personal about the recruiter. Look for some common thread that will break the ice and form rapport with the interviewer. Are there any items in the room that are similar to your interests? During one interview I had, the recruiter had a replica of a NASCAR race car and being the racing enthusiast I am, I immediately keyed in on this and it became an ice breaker. When you introduce yourself, have a smile and a firm handshake and this applies to females as well. Don't pretend you are Mr. Universe and crush their hand or offer limp handshakes, whether male or female. Offering a limp handshake indicates a lack of confidence on your part. As you grip their hand make sure the web between the thumb and finger interlock. Slightly tilt your hand towards theirs as you grab hold. This will give a solid grasp. Do not sit down until you are invited to do so, and at least after the interviewer have taken their seat. If they do not point you to any particular chair, take the seat that allows sufficient space between you.

Most times the interview will be at their desk so a chair on the opposite side is appropriate. If you have been invited to sit with them at a conference table, allow them the seat at the head of the table and take the first one on either side. Make sure when you sit down that your chair is facing the interviewer and if you need to move the chair ask the interviewer for permission. You may be offered a beverage of sort, but it is best to politely decline it. No matter how careful you normally are, this will be the time you will spill it and no doubt, it will land on either the interviewer or the papers in front of him. Throughout the interview, continually make eye contact but don't leer at them. This will only make them nervous and uncomfortable.

Make sure you use the interviewers name often. It is not necessary to use it each time you address them but make it obvious you are aware of who they are but do not attempt to take control of the interviewer. Let the interviewer be in control or they will see you as too domineering. Keep eye contact often but do not stare. If you do not maintain eye contact it may signify boredom on your part. I remember an old saying that farmers did not trust anyone who would not look them in the eye. Of course even if someone looks you in the eye it does not mean they are honest but the likelihood is in your favor. Focus on what the interviewer is saying. Sit with your back straight and against the back of the chair but slightly lean forward. It gives the impression that you are focused on what they are saying. It is most acceptable to take notes during the interview but make sure you have some form of presentable or professional portfolio. It is advisable to ask permission first.

Throughout the interview be conscious of any annoying habits such as tapping your pen, slouching or a constantly twitching leg. These habits not only indicate nervousness but a lack of confidence. Some females have a habit of twirling their hair while they are speaking or males may play with their mustache. Another habit that is common is the candidate sits there with their arms folded across their chest indicating boredom as well. Waving both your hands when you talk happens when you are very nervous so be conscious of it. You want to exhibit as much confidence as possible. Speaking too fast or failing to make eye contact are ways to get the interviewer to lose focus. Your body language says a lot. Your body may be saying things that you do not intend. Showing good body language will help to put the interviewer at ease. It will indicate confidence on your part. These are things that can be corrected during your pre interview practice.

If you are over the age of 50, you may be concerned about this fact. There are ways to get around it. As you sit with the interviewer, direct them to a discussion that will enable you to present your skills and how they can satisfy the needs of the company. This will provide you with an opportunity at the end of the interview to revert back to your presentation and ask them how they felt about it. Some candidates make an attempt to work around or hide their age. This is not necessary; you give the interviewer the opportunity to be as concerned about your age as you are. I recently heard of an example of someone explaining being overqualified. In 2009, you may remember the US Airways plane that ditched in the river in New York City. That pilot had years of experience and could be classified as being overqualified. Because of the circumstances in how it played out, would you have wanted anyone else less qualified if you were a passenger on that plane?

Interviews can sometimes be over lunch or dinner and there are some extra concerns should this happen. Watch what types of food you order, otherwise you may look foolish. Ordering spaghetti and having sauce splashed over your nice white starched shirt or white blouse sends a bad signal. I have seen friends humiliate themselves eating lobster or spare ribs. Although these may be foods that you love, the interview is more important now. Just take small bites and chew quietly. As far as table etiquette, keep your fork in your left hand with the knife in your right hand. Move any dirty dishes and utensils out of the way. If this is to be a working lunch, then make sure the surface is clean so as to avoid any spills on your paperwork. Also avoid ordering any foods that require you to eat with your hands such as hamburgers or corn on the cob. If you order salad, avoid celery or other noisy food as this becomes too distracting. The subject of liquor may come up and this could be used as a test. Avoid it even if your dinner partner partakes of it because you will need to be on your toes and liquor, or "truth serum" as I call it, can put you into an embarrassing situation. When you are ordering, don't think that just because they are picking up the tab that you can order what you want. Allow your dinner partner to order first and then take their lead. If they order a salad then don't order the Filet Mignon.

Once the food has arrived your discussion is well into the interview process and it is not necessary to stop talking but a word of caution..do not talk with your mouth full. You will only shoot yourself in the foot if very unexpectedly a morsel of food flies out of your mouth. Of course, if you eat before you arrive at the interview, be careful on what you eat, especially with the odors that accompany some food. I think back to the scene in the movie "Pretty Woman" where Julia Roberts thrusts a piece of food out of her mouth, only to be caught by the server. Make sure you are courteous to all of the servers. Being rude with them sends a negative message to the interviewer. This could be your interviewer's favorite restaurant and if you embarrass them, most likely you won't be having lunch with this interviewer again.

Speak loud enough for the interviewer to hear but not those in the office next door and don't talk too fast. Those from New England, such as me, have a tendency to speak faster than those in the south. If you add your nervousness to this fast talk then the interviewer can become confused. During any of your conversations there should be no negative talk about your previous employer or boss. Once this door opens, Pandora's Box has opened and there may be no return. Of course you should be listening much more than you speak. Again, let the interviewer control the flow of the conversation. A strong word of caution in that do not exhibit any signs of negativity, no matter what you thought of the previous company or boss. This will only give the impression you are the problem and not your previous employer. They are not interested in the fact that you were "wronged" in your last position. Just show a great amount of passion and turn any negatives into positives. A winning interview will be made up of the following:

- An energetic, enthusiastic and smiling candidate
- Be yourself and be relaxed
- Don't be arrogant but do be humble
- Be prepared with questions for the interviewer
- Make a connection with the interviewer

Your interview will be made up of questions, whether behavioral or functional. Preparation and practice is what it will take to be successful during this interview step. The best method to answer the question is the SAR method. Situation, Action and

Results will be the key to providing a thorough answer. This method is sometimes known as S.T.A.R. with the T representing Task. Either method will provide the interviewer with an in depth answer to the question. Let's review an example of a response to an interviewer's question. The interviewer has asked you about a time when you were faced with a problem and how you reacted to it. Your reply could be as follows:

"I was confronted at my last job with a time that our computer system went down due to a local experienced television cable contractor having cut some underground lines during construction. It was estimated that it would take 4-6 hours to repair the line. As each call center representative needed their computer and a phone to complete their duties, it was necessary to restructure the process so that employees were not forced to lose time. I had each supervisor assign a portion of the alphabet to each representative for reviewing updates to our vendor profiles. The project was scheduled to commence 30 days later so this enabled us to come out ahead of schedule. Once the system came back up, on a volunteer system we created a second shift to make up for the lost calls during the downtime. By the end of the month we actually had made up all lost time and completed the project 30 days in advance."

See how the SAR process worked? It stated the problem (situation) and what action you took and the results from it. What this showed is how you reacted under pressure thus giving some indication of how you would act in future situations. A very good indicator of future behavior is past behavior. It will indicate to the interviewer you can react to unprepared occurrences during your work day. We all know that no matter what your profession is, problems happen. What you do not want to do during this process is bore the interviewer with a long, drawn out response. Over-answering the questions presented to you will have a negative effect. Keep your answers to their questions brief and to the point. This will keep the interviewer in tune with you and allow more time to showcase all of your talents. But let me add a caveat here…do not be too curt in your replies.

You do want to make sure you are answering the question fully and in a way that the interviewer will understand.

Remember that they are not in your profession and may not understand all the elements of your job. For example, if you are in management you will, without a doubt, be asked if you have supervised other employees. Just replying yes will not fully answer their question. Explain how many you supervised and in what capacity. If you tell them you have supervised people and give no further details, either they will be annoyed at the lack of response or they will move on assuming your supervisory experience was minimal. And if you had supervised a large team of 100 employees for a period of two years are you not doing an injustice to yourself? Take the extra time and satisfy their concerns by giving full details, concise and to the point.

Make sure you fully understand the question before you answer it and listen to the question before you begin answering. You may want to repeat the question back to the interviewer to ensure you have full understood the question. In addition, sit back and think about the response for a few seconds. The interviewer will understand that you need a few seconds to get your thoughts together. Taking this time will help you prepare for the best answer and possibly save the interview. Providing the most accurate and detailed answer is what you want. Obviously you will be practicing answering questions prior to your interview. You won't know what questions will be asked so some preparation will not be possible however you may be asked some questions that you will expect or have practiced. Make sure your answers are your own and not word for word from a book. The interviewer has heard all the answers and if your response is what they heard from the last candidate, your goose is cooked. Most questions can be answered by thoughtful, common sense.

You may find it arise during an interview as to whether or not you are overqualified for the position. Some are subtle about it and others will come right out and question you. When this happens, redirect the question back at them by asking them to explain why they think that. Be ready to offer the fact that you bring much experience and that it will only help to alleviate some of the pressure or stress they are facing. Hiring you will provide them valuable time to address other issues whereas they will not have to micro manage you.

Asking questions at an interview is not a one sided affair. It is your duty and responsibility to ask questions of the interviewer. They most likely expect it and will probably be disappointed if you do not ask any. This may signify to them that you are not very interested in the position or the company. Most interviewers assume you have done your research about the company and will be expecting some questions. Do not disappoint them and besides if you are interested in the position, would you not want more details than what is in the job description that was posted for the ad? Prepare several questions ahead of time, prior to the interview. You can bring them with you and look at them during the question segment of the interview. There will be no concern from the interviewer and probably happiness that you will ask them questions. Below are some examples of questions you could ask. Obviously you will have some additional ones after you perform you due diligence on the company.

- What are the strengths and weaknesses of this company?
- What kind of training do you provide for this position?
- Why is this position available?
- Is there continued training?
- What are the responsibilities of this position?
- Who would I report to?
- Is there a job description I could see for this position?
- How is my performance reviewed and when?
- What do you (interviewer) like best about this company?
- What happened to the last person in this position?
- Does the company promote from within?
- What is the culture of the organization?
- What are the challenges or problems facing the candidate in this position?

I again repeat…make sure you ask questions. Don't just sit there like a lump on a log. If you do this, then you wasted your time and theirs even showing up for the interview. This will signify you are not a friendly person nor will you mingle well with the current employees. As you are sitting there, make sure your posture is good. When you sit down, place your lower back solid against the back of the chair. Sit erect with your shoulders straight and do not fold your arms. This is a habit that many people have but comes across negative to the interviewer. It will indicate a form of boredom and again it could doom you. Make sure as you ask and answer the questions that you articulate your words and speak very clearly. And watch how you answer each of those questions presented to you. When you are asked about you last supervisor, telling the interviewer that he/she was an idiot is not going to win you any points. This will instantly tell them you may be hard to deal with and are not a valid candidate, even if your last supervisor was an idiot. You have got to show a good attitude during the process. You can do your homework and show up prepared but showing the wrong attitude is a bullet in the foot.

Many times you can answer questions based on your findings from reviewing the company mission and vision statements. This usually will indicate the current culture of the interviewing organization. You will have a better idea of what to expect at the interview. It may indicate they are dedicated to great customer service and this is your forte. You can build your questions and answers around this knowledge.

We've covered many of the questions that you can ask and those that can be asked of you. But there are questions that the interviewer cannot ask. They are illegal and designated as too personal and not relevant to the position. Sometimes the interviewer has no ulterior motive when asking these questions but none the less it still does not compensate for asking illegal questions. Then again, there are interviewers that may present trick questions that have a way of getting into personal information. If you find you are being asked personal questions and you feel you did not get the position based on the answers to these questions contact your local Equal Employment Opportunity Council (EEOC) office. You may have grounds for a lawsuit. I was once asked the question "What would you do if you were king of the world." At the end of the interview I asked the interviewer his reasoning for that question. He stated to me that questions like this often give him details that he cannot ask. Although a creative way, I would question the legality of his intentions.

Below are some examples of illegal questions.

- How old are you?
- Do you have children?
- What nationality are you?
- Are you married?
- Do you have arrangements made for childcare?
- What religion are you?
- Where were you born?

Keep in mind that the interviewer has a position to fill and they want to fill it as soon as possible with the best candidate. As you will have certain responsibilities when you accept the position, this is one of theirs. The point here is that they have a vested interest in you; otherwise you would not be sitting in that seat. They want you to do good so they can forward you on to the hiring manager. Do not try to read the interviewer during the process to see if you stand a chance or not. A good interviewer will give you no indication of whether you are a solid candidate or not. Simply go through the process doing the best you can. If you sit there worried about each question on how you did, you will not perform well and again will eliminate your odds.

The first question you are apt to hear during the interview is "Tell me about yourself". This is a good time to give your elevator speech which you have practiced so hard on. It sums up your direction as well as gives a good idea of what you have done in the past. The elevator speech should be periodically reviewed and adjusted slightly. The reason is that you may encounter the same people at multiple networking events and a little change in your speech will not bore them. They may have heard it two or three times in the last week or so at other networking events. Also, it gives you a chance to continue improving it. In addition, based on the possibility that you may interview for positions somewhat dissimilar, variation becomes necessary. Don't forget to practice it in front on a mirror and preferably with a tape recorder.

SAMPLE ELEVATOR SPEECH

"Hello, my name is John Doe and I have over twenty years experience in inventory control at the Director level. Most recently I was employed as Director of Inventory Control for XYZ Company. My vast experience includes consumer goods, automobile inventory, as well as manufacturing. I am seeking a position as a VP or Director of Inventory Control in the Boston area but am open to other major cities such as Chicago or Atlanta. I've been recognized for reducing inventory shrinkage by 25%."

You will notice that the emphasis is "I" here, not we. You may be a great team builder and your success has centered on what your team has provided but this is not the time to brag about your employees. They are not at the interview,.. you are, so take advantage of it. Everything you talk about needs to showcase your talents. Emphasize your people skills such as being a team player, motivational techniques, leadership, flexibility, agreeableness, and that you are a good listener. Divert yourself from your resume because they know your qualifications. Your resume has them listed and that same resume got you this interview. Perhaps you could mention other skills such as problem solving skills, showing your logic, creativity, and that you are capable of developing solutions that will serve purpose for the company. In addition, establish some groundwork that shows your strategic planning capabilities, preferably with some examples. What you want to do is tell them in your own words that you can fix their problems. Keep in mind there is a difference between bragging and showing your confidence. If you step over this line and it appears that you are just flooding them with unsubstantiated bragging, you have failed the interview. They want someone who is confident and in control, especially if this is for a position of leadership.

Practicing answering questions prior to the interview should eliminate this. By focusing on what you have accomplished during your career you will give them a wonderful overview of your abilities. Get away from the word for word declarations on your resume. Get to the meat of what you have done and put it in your own words. You need to locate ways to be different from your competition for the job. What can you say that will separate yourself from the last candidate the recruiter interviewed? You can indicate you are a great multi-tasker but give some examples. Just telling them won't impress them but facts will.

If there are occurrences of job hopping on your resume do not bring it up at the interview but do not avoid it if the interviewer does ask. Have a good explanation about why there are numerous jobs. It may be something simple as restructuring or downsizing which most recruiters will understand. I caution you to tell the truth and do not lie about it. But what you can do is present it in a positive note. Prove to the interviewer that you will make a good fit for the position. They are sitting there waiting for this from you. Convince them you are the solution to their problems. You must sell yourself, not just sit back and wait for their questions. Ask for the job! Tell them you want to use your experience and qualifications to help advance their company. Ask them what you can offer to put you at an advantage to get this job. They will tell you most of the time. Ask them if there is any reason you are not the top candidate for this position. It may give you an opportunity to clear up any concerns they have.

There are a couple of other types of interviews that you need to be prepared for. The first is a telephone interview. You have to prepare for this just as you would for a face to face interview. Make sure you get dressed and not sit there with your pajamas and slippers on. If you dress up you will feel better and will handle yourself better as well. Sit at your desk showing good posture as if you were sitting in front of a recruiter. You should even consider standing up as it helps you breath better. Have notes available to ask the interviewer. On several phone interviews I have had, I had pasted numerous Post It notes all over my computer in preparation. I was able to quickly ask questions or make statements. As I finished each question, I removed it. Make sure you have a copy of your resume handy as well. They may ask you certain questions such as dates of employment and with a resume handy you will be better prepared. And above all, smile. An interviewer can always tell when you are or are not smiling.

Before you hang up the phone, get their name and contact information to follow up with them in a couple of days. This contact information should include an email address at the very least. Keep a connection to them open. As you talk with them, make sure you talk slow and clear. Telephones have a way of muffling a conversation. This could lead to a face to face interview. Of course, do not chew gum or smoke during the telephone interview. This is distracting both to you and the interviewer. Avoid coughing in the phone and if it does happen, then cover the phone.

Panel interviews are another form that you may encounter. A panel interview is where you may appear before several people at one time. It may be that you are applying for a VP of Lending position and will have to appear before several department heads that may include the CFO, VP of Collections, etc. Do not let this intimidate you. As you are presented questions from each panel member respond to their questions as if you are only speaking to them but make sure you look at each of the members of the panel and continue to have good eye contact throughout the interview. They may have had this same question on their mind so they will be alert to your answers. As you answer their question use their name so it gives the impression you are directing your replies solely to them. You will see a variety of questions and attitudes as each person is different and will be looking for certain patterns from you.

You may also encounter chain interviews where you will most likely have the interview with the HR representative, followed by representatives of other departments similar to the panel interview but on a one-on-one basis. You may be brought to each of their departments or they could be called in to the interview room one at a time. Either way, do not let it make you nervous and answer their questions with clarity and confidence. As you meet with each individual of these areas, make it a point to tactfully strategically align yourself with them. Consider that each person is an individual "battle" and if you win all of the battles, you win the war. You will have to make adjustments along the way as each of them will undoubtedly have different personalities.

One dilemma that has faced many job candidates is how to answer that famous comment from interviewers "You are overqualified." If you do not respond to this immediately, you also will be one of those walking out the door for the last time. The interviewer may be just presenting this to you to see your reaction or maybe just to eliminate another candidate. Come right back at them, confidently and politely, by asking "Why do you think that?" It now puts them on the spot and they will be forced to respond and then you can satisfy them with an appropriate answer. One reply from you might be "Mr. Employer, what was it that interested you about me enough to bring me in for an interview? Do you really think I am overqualified?" "Do you not think the qualities I offer will provide an excellent solution to your problems?" Go on further by asking them what their ideal candidate looks like. Ask them if they have any concerns over your ability to do the job. These replies will now direct them into further conversation and the opportunity to showcase your abilities. You want to be the last person on their mind and this could get you there. This instance provides you with an excellent opportunity to show your level of confidence. Use it to your full advantage.

The question of salary evokes chills up ones spine. Too often the question comes up about your salary expectations and you must be prepared on how to respond. Before the interview you should research similar positions to see what the market is for that same position. One good source is Salary.com. Most positions are listed here so you will at least have a range of what the position may offer. Do not be the one who brings up the salary question at the interview. Whoever brings it up first loses. Let them make the first move and be assured it will come about. If they ask you what your salary expectations are, be prepared with your desired as well as your bottom line amount. Question them on what the salary range is and whether that is the hiring range or the employed range. You may find the following reply helpful:

"I am looking for an opportunity to showcase my talents. I am quite sure a progressive company such as yours will make me a good offer. What is the salary range for the _____ position?"

Some organizations have two different ranges. You may get backed into the corner and have to offer a figure. If not and the question comes up, advise the interviewer that you are confident that their company will make a respectable offer to someone with your excellent qualifications. Find a way to deflect the question and ask them the range. However the question comes up, be prepared in advance as this is one of the most important issues that will arise. It will be your starting point with that company and that won't change. Try to give a range rather than a solid figure. It will give you some negotiating room. If they say that your range is too high, simply tell them "My results with my current/past employer encouraged them to put me in this range. I am quite sure you would want the same outstanding results from me."

When an offer has been made, no matter how you feel about it, ask them for a couple of days to think about it. Do not accept or refuse immediately. It may put them on defense and if they want you bad enough they will be considering a higher figure. How you play it after that point will result in the final decision. Think about the offer for a couple of days and consider everything that goes with it such as benefits and whether they offer tuition reimbursement or relocation assistance. If relocation is required, you want to know what your new expenses will be such as rent or mortgage payments. Perhaps housing is more expensive in this new area. Will you need to buy new suits because your old job was business casual attire? Are the group medical insurance premiums higher? Consider all your potential expenses. Once you accept their offer, ask them for it in writing. An acquaintance of mine interviewed several times for a VP position with the CEO and during the process the CEO retired and a new CEO was hired before the candidate was hired. Now, fortunately the candidate was not offered a salary before they left but what if they had and it was oral. The question is whether the new CEO would have made the same offer?

Do not be afraid to negotiate salary or benefits. Maybe the salary is not what you expected so can the deal be made sweeter by securing more vacation time or relocation costs? There may be other benefits you can negotiate for such as quicker vesting time in insurance or retirement programs. But before you negotiate any salary make sure you know exactly what your job duties will be. You don't want any surprises and look back and regret the decision you made. Keep in mind what is the best situation for your entire family.

Make sure you have practiced your closure skills by exhibiting passion for their company as well as the position being offered. Summarize what you can do for the company and how you can solve their problem. Use your own words and terminology in your summation but watch how you use industry terminology. If you are speaking using terminology unfamiliar to the recruiter, you will confuse them. Not all human resources professionals know the industry jargon. If you are unsuccessful in getting this position ask them if they have other positions that match your background and qualifications. Recently a friend of mine had applied for one position but after interviewing several times, the company found she was overqualified and in the end offered her a position that was more senior than the last position, with obviously higher salary.

If you are still a candidate for the position, do not go home and sit back expecting a call offering you the position. Continue looking because you do not know what the outcome will be, no matter how well you did at the interview. Too often I have seen candidates leave the interview feeling extremely confident only to go home and sit at the beach for the next couple of days waiting for the offer to come. Unfortunately it never did.

Now the interview has ended and you have all of your questions answered. Before you leave, thank the interviewer for their time and consideration. Let them know you appreciate the opportunity to have interviewed with them. Shake their hand and ask them for their business card and keep that smile on your face. This is their last impression of you so make it good. Don't ask them how you did during the interview but do ask them if you can follow up with them and offer a time and date when you will. As you leave, thank the gatekeeper as well. They may have further discussions with the hiring party about you. Leave a good impression with them as well.

Once you arrive home, sit down immediately and make any notes about the position while they are still fresh in your mind. Then handwrite a thank you note not only to the interviewer but the gatekeeper as well and walk them to the mailbox. If you are near a post office deposit them in the receptacle there. You want the interviewer to get the thank you note as soon as possible. They will appreciate the prompt action as well as the handwritten note or card. If there was something personal about the interviewer that you learned, make mention of it. For example there may have been a special piece of art in their office or you may have discussed the college their child was going to. This will impress them and make them realize you were listening to everything they had to offer. You may also use this card to address any concerns the interviewer had about hiring you. It is even permissible and suggested that you send a customized letter to the interviewer.

Obviously thank them for their time but add something further about your career that did not come up during the interview. Let them know you are extremely interested in the job. Write the letter with the assumption you are a strong candidate. You may even go so far as letting them know you will follow up with them in a few days or week. After a few days it is time to follow up with the interviewer to see if any decision has been made. Hopefully you obtained their business card when you left so that you have all the necessary contact information. Preferably, call them and request some response on the status of the hiring decision. This will just get your name fresh in their mind and perhaps it could be a deciding factor. Maybe you were on even keel with another candidate and they failed to follow-up. Little things like this make the difference. Do not miss any opportunities to keep in touch. Obviously, you do not want to hound them every day. Make your first call two or three days after the interview. If you end up leaving a voice message and do not get a response that day or the next, again call them. Be polite on your calls and messages. If you do get to speak with them and no decision has been made, ask them when they anticipate a decision being made. If they say next Tuesday, then on Wednesday, pick up the phone and call them on that day. If you just sit back and wait for their call, who knows when it will come.

By making these attempts, you have signified you want the job and won't give up until you have it. Again, you do not want to call them every day for a week. This will only annoy them and perhaps assist them in making the decision, and not the way you had hoped. If they do become annoyed they will most likely let you know they will get back with you when a decision is made and it is unnecessary for you to call them until that time. This may be the appropriate signal to back off for a few days. Perhaps an email will be necessary at the end of the specified time. This will have to be a decision depending on your rapport with them.

"Be courageous! Have Faith! Go forward!"
-Thomas Edison

9.
ENTREPRENEURSHIP

THIS CHAPTER WILL COVER BEING AN ENTREPRENEUR, DEFINED IN Webster's dictionary as "one who organizes a business undertaking, assuming the risk for the sake of the profit." I do not plan on spending a lot of time discussing this. Not because it is not a viable option, but that there are so many books and magazines out there that will cover this in much more detail. I would like to emphasize that it is a viable option, one that deserves serious consideration, whether you are currently employed or not. If you are successful in this venture, you will find that your confidence and self esteem will improve.

Being an entrepreneur does not necessarily require multitudes of money. There are many home based businesses' that can be started with minimal funds. At the time I researched the material for this book, I had a friend that bought into an online travel agency with less than a thousand dollars. It just depends on what you want to do and whether this is going to be a part time business or your full time vocation. There are sources out there such as magazines, business brokers and franchise companies that will provide you with an array of opportunities. Before you do get far into the dream, first decide why you want to be self-employed. Is it just a whim or do you have a deep passion for it? You will need your emotions to support you throughout the process, not just in founding the business but continuing to keep it running.

Purchase one of the magazines at your local supermarket or book store and get some ideas that are available. These magazines will only cover franchise opportunities but they may get the juices flowing and you may come up with your own idea. As part of your research, first determine what you like to do or what you are capable of doing. Do you have a hobby that could evolve into something? For example, are you an avid photographer? How many professional photographers out there do you think got their start from it being their hobby? Perhaps you are into woodcraft and are quite good at it. This could also evolve into something special. Many times I have been out for a ride and seen hand crafted lawn chairs or lawn ornaments for sale. This probably was the result of someone's hobby. Are you so good with the nine-iron that perhaps offering golf lessons part time is a possibility? There are so many hobbies that we engage in on a daily basis that could support your efforts into full and part time business ventures.

Obviously, financial considerations are a key factor in what you will do. If the savings account says no, then purchasing a McDonalds franchise is out of the question. This will take hundreds of thousands of dollars. You may want to visit your local Small Business Administration (SBA) office to get some counseling. There are many programs available, especially for minority groups. You may find that you qualify for loans that will get you the necessary funds to open up a business and it does not necessarily have to be a franchise. Your local newspaper will have a section in the classifieds that advertise local businesses for sale and most of them are not franchise opportunities. Do make sure, before you throw yourself into the process that you do your homework and ensure that you will have proper backing and support from the franchise owners. Whether it is a franchise or not, it is suggested you also investigate the company to see how successful they are. You certainly do not want to invest in a company only to find out they are on the verge of bankruptcy or that their building lease has expired and is non-renewable. The Service Corps of Retired Executives, (S.C.O.R.E.) works in partnership with the SBA and provides services to those just starting out in business. This is an excellent organization and has been around since 1964 and provides one on one meetings with the new entrepreneur.

Visit www.sba.gov or www.score.gov.

Before you undertake any kind of business venture look inside yourself and determine if you are truly committed to this venture and whether you have the discipline to make it work. Most business' fail within the first two years, and if there is a lack of commitment or discipline, you only make the odds greater that you will fail. You do have three options on which way to go if you are business bound: start-ups, existing business, or a franchise. Assuming you do have the commitment, there are many rewards from owning your own company. Obviously you are more in control of your destiny. No one is going to be waiting at the time clock on Friday afternoon with a pink slip. Those businesses' that do make it past the two year incubation period have greater chances of becoming truly successful. You may realize more income than you could ever imagine and the possibility of passing down the business to your family certainly has to rank right at the top. This provides you with a sense of satisfaction that you cannot receive working for someone else. Most of us would like to pass down some form of legacy and this is one option to make that happen.

But remember that owning a business is not a 9-5 job, nor is there a guaranteed paycheck each week. Most business owners spend twice that amount of time working at making their business successful. And when the rest of the family wants to go to the beach on Saturday morning, it most likely will not be possible for you. It takes hard work and long hours, so put some intense thinking into this before you make the move. You can't just quit with a two week notice. During this thinking process determine what your fears are. Is it financial, the long hours, the commitment needed or your lack of experience? Once you determine all your fears, you need to decide if they are founded or not. One obstacle you will most certainly face is the negative feedback you will receive from friends and relatives. You must avoid this because this is a sure way to drop your dream. Do not allow them to pull you down. Now, there will be some legitimate concerns that they will bring up. Some of these friends and relatives will probably have the knowledge and firsthand experience that could offer you some great experience. On the flip side, once you have your business up and running and have become established in the community, there is more flexibility of time with your family. Properly run companies can allow the owner to take extra time off that may not have been possible in the corporate world.

Once you overcome your fears and have researched what direction you want to take, then take the necessary steps and move forward or perhaps drop the dream. You may realize that you are better suited for being an employee rather than an employer. And perhaps you will realize what you are best suited for and who knows, you may realize from all of your research that not only are you best suited to be an employee but that you may decide to change occupations. As of this writing, the state of the economy in the United States was the worse it had been since the 1930s. Many experts feel that the main force in rebounding will be the small mom and pop type of operations, not the large corporations. If this is true, this could be the right time to start up that business. There is funding available in spite of the economic problems that surround us.

The financial aspect of running a business does not stop with the money necessary to purchase the business. You must have sufficient cash for the long haul. You still have to support your family as well as have funds for the expenses that surround a business, such as payroll, modernizing of equipment, supplies needed to run the business and funds necessary to offset losses sustained. When you prepare your business plan, this must be taken into account. If you are unfamiliar with business plans, now is the time to look into how to prepare one. Your local community college may offer courses in preparing business plans. Other local civic organizations may also offer courses for a modest fee to educate you.

Business plans provide a synopsis of the proposed company's direction as well as its objective. It will state what products you will sell or the services you will provide. Included is a brief marketing plan covering pricing and marketing of the product or service. There will be a discussion on who the officers are and how many employees will be needed, now and in the future. Furthermore, there will be a financial strategy outlined. It will also discuss where your funding will come from and what cash flow will be needed. There is minimal income the first two years you are open. This is a crucial time especially for the financial aspect of it. Can you support your family for up to two years on savings?

If you decide to go the way of a franchise, you should find that their corporate office will supply you with intensive training. Any of the top franchises out there will offer some form of training. It will be paid by you in most cases, but it will give you a solid start to being successful. The training is usually at the corporate office so you will get firsthand knowledge of the entire operation. And remember, these are the professionals. It is their area of expertise and they know all of the pitfalls and how to either avoid them or overcome them. Dig into this deeply and make sure that you are prepared to open the doors correctly. You will need to research the area you want to start the business. Look into crime statistics, unemployment, have other business' failed in this location. You will also want to make sure the market is not saturated with competition, who may be well established in the area.

There are several options of how you can open a new business venture. You could create an Limited Liability Corporation, known as an LLC. Partnerships or just a Sole Proprietorship as well as forming a corporation are just a couple of other options. You need to look into the pro's and con's of each form of business.

In summarizing entrepreneurship, you must spend time researching everything about it from the emotional side to the financial side. Make sure this is the direction that you want to go in and that you will have the support not only of your family, but of those associated with the business. Will your community provide you with support, not only emotional but is there a need for this type of business. Starting a snow plowing business in Orlando, Florida is just a ridiculous choice. On the other side, opening up a landscaping business in Boston, Massachusetts requires equally much thought. The weather, climate, the housing industry, age of the community and the growth of the community are but only a few of the things to be aware of. There are cities and towns in the United States that have actually reduced in population over the last 10 years. Is this a factor in the business you wish to pursue? Without a doubt it is. Do your homework and spend time with your family discussing this move. If you put the necessary thought and research into it, you will make the correct decision.

"Believe in your strength and your vision. Learn to repeat to yourself, 'It all depends on me."

-Andre Gide

10.
GOAL SETTING

Get yourself in gear.

Orchestrate the direction of your life.

Advance the quality of your life.

Live life to your fullest potential.

Strategize where your future will take you.

GOALS...THE FUNDAMENTAL BASIS FOR SUCCESS AND YOU CAN BE the one to choose them and direct their path. I remember reading once how someone described goals; "You don't have to have goals. You can always choose to serve as a pitiful example." Although this statement may be a little strong, it does make quite the valid point. Goals serve as a roadmap for your life. They give you direction and serve as a critique of where you have been. Most people will say they have goals but question them a little and you will find that it is rarely true. I have done this many times and usually the only time I get a solid answer is from those individuals who are successful in their lives. Does this mean they are millionaires or drive a Ferrari? Certainly not, as that is not the basis for goals, although each of these items may be on the list of those having goals. We'd all like to be rich and drive a fancy sports car but just "wishing" it will happen rarely accomplishes the end result we are seeking. Goals keep you focused on the task at hand.

    You cannot just list a series of goals and stuff them in your desk drawer. You must put a plan in place to achieve them. Goals will direct your energy in the right direction and you will find that goals will improve your attitude towards life in your daily process. They will assist you by improving your daily performance both in your personal life as well as career. Not only will they help your personal career but you will quickly find that they will be beneficial to any team member that you lead in your career. And if your team is successful in their goals, whose career will these goals also enhance? As you and your team progress in your goals, they will inspire each of you in providing added confidence and creating even more intensity.

We have talked a little about goals throughout this book but I felt that it was appropriate to dedicate an entire chapter to goals and goal setting. Whether you are unemployed or just looking to make an employment change matters little to whether you should have goals or not. Goals should be a necessary part of your daily life and they must be those goals that you believe in. You most likely have goals but may have never sat down and put them on paper. This should be your initial task and close monitoring of these goals should be an everyday happening in your life. You should set a part of your day aside, whether it is early morning or after dinner. Find a quiet spot and sit down and review them. It will take you several drafts before you actually find the ones that are most important to you. In the next paragraph we will delve into the process. These goals should cover all aspects of your life from financial to personal development. Other areas are family time, religious and spiritual, fitness and health. Within each of these categories are many sub-goals that only you can determine. As you sit down and write out your drafts, most of your questions will be answered. You may even find that you have had several of these goals but not only did you not write them down, but you tucked them in the back of your mind.

Goals must follow the following five parameters. Note that the acronym, coined by Ken Blanchard, for the foundation of the process is S.M.A.R.T.

- Specific...Each goal must be explicit and indicate in precise terms what the goal is so that anyone who looks at it will know what it is.
- Measurable...The goal must be able to be measured and the content having some form of dimensions.
- Action..The goal should present a plan of action or direction.

- **R**ealistic..Each goal must hold the sense it can be accomplished.
- **T**ime Bound..One cannot truly have goals without having some boundaries or parameters such as a calendar date.

Before we go into each category, let me emphasize that goals must have serious thought put into them. Just sitting down and jotting five or six goals on paper with little thought or a plan doesn't provide you with the direction where you really want to go or the results that you should achieve. It is a painstaking process that should be well thought out. Get a pencil and paper and first sit down and think about the areas of your life which you would like to see improved. As mentioned previously, these categories should encompass religious or spiritual areas, education, career direction, and family oriented or personal goals such as weight loss or running a marathon. It may be that you want to become a member of a community group such as Habitat for Humanity or joining the Lions Club. You may want to have financial goals as part of the plan. Look at the areas of your life that you are not happy with or feel that you have not accomplished everything you wanted. Once you have listed everything, then this will be the time to fine tune them. You will find that after you list your initial goals, that your direction will slightly change and you will become more focused on what you want and probably less generalized. Keep in mind that as you look to fine tune them, decide if it is a goal that you really need or want. It may be just a wild dream that you know will never happen. For example, stating you want to win the state lottery may not be the most intelligent goal. We would all like to win the lottery but we have very little control over it other than buying a ticket.

There is a wonderful quotation that serves as a good interlude for goals:

"Goals provide the energy that powers our lives. One of the best ways we can get the most from energy we have is to focus it. That is what goals can do for us: concentrate our energy."

-Denis Waitley

Let's look at each one individually starting with specifics. An example of a goal that is not specific is a businessman stating he wants to be successful. What does that mean? How about a tourist stating he wants to go on a vacation. What does that tell you? Very little indeed! Now let's put each into a specific goal. The businessman or CEO in this case may state he wants to increase the profit of his company 5% over the previous year's results. The tourist may state they want to go to California to see the San Diego Zoo. Now, doesn't this give you a better idea of what is in each person's mind? You may think your first goal should be to look better but that is not specific enough. Although it is a great first goal, put some thought into it and state you want to lose some weight. How much or how soon does not have to be part of the specific category. This will be addressed in the other categories.

Measurable goals take into consideration how you can track the success of each one. Relating to your goal of losing weight, here is where you can state how much weight you wish to lose. By stating that you want to lose 10 pounds, you have indicated just how much weight you wish to lose so at the end of your goal period, you are able to realize whether you accomplished your goal or not. Your goal may be running a race, so state that you want to run in the Boston Marathon, as a marathon is just over 26 miles. But that could be a long range goal and if you are not an avid runner now, then perhaps the first goal should be is to run a 5K, just over 3 miles. Although the marathon is measurable, it could serve as a deterrent in the long run. I say this because it will be harder to establish the time bound factors on this goal if you are not running regularly. By setting the smaller race goal (5K) first and then upon accomplishing that, increasing it to a 10K, you will be less frustrated not seeing results you expected.

Being action bound gives the goal some foundation. Go into detail on your specific goal. It might have to do with the training regimen of running a 5K or marathon. It could be that you are running every day at 5 am or late evening, whatever time you choose to run. You could take into consideration how you would run in inclement weather. If you live in the northeast, then a plan

B should be set so when you wake up to a foot of snow you will not lose any ground. If you are an afternoon runner and you live in Florida, then perhaps you should also have a secondary plan to adjust for those days when the thermometer hits 90+ degrees. Plan B does not have to be part of the actual goal but a backup plan in your mind to avoid those bumps in the road. In each of the examples above, just knowing you have a treadmill in your den enables you to continue with your target. Now, if you do not have a treadmill and cannot afford one at this time, allow for that as you set your goal. If you live in New England, you know you will get snow in the winter, etc.

The goal must be realistic and not just a pipe dream. Stating that you want to run the Boston Marathon next month when you have not run in 10 years is not realistic. You will soon abandon the goal or even worse, injure yourself trying to accomplish the goal. On the other hand, make sure the goal is not so far out that you will lose interest. If you run regularly and have run in marathons in the past, then do not state you want to run in the Boston Marathon 10 years down the road. It is too far out and better you establish another goal that may relate to running. Stating that you want to play for the Los Angeles Lakers and although you were a great basketball player in college 20 years ago, lets face it, you are "too old" to make the team. I mean no disrespect but remember that basketball players are usually thinking of retiring at the ripe "old" age of 35.

As far as time bound, this is the last element of establishing a goal. Using the weight goal, we can set a time bound goal of losing the ten pounds by an established date. It may be 45 days down the road but you have established a time table which will give you a date to shoot for and an element that will assist you in determining if you accomplished your goal as you originally set it. One point I would like to mention is that any element of the five goal-setting parameters can be changed at any time. It is not cheating to alter the goal as you go along. For example, let's say your goal was to run a 5K race within sixty days, however two weeks out you fell down and injured yourself to a point that the doctor prohibits any running for 90 days. Obviously the chances of accomplishing your goal are next to zero. Just alter the date once you are able to go back to running. Perhaps you were too aggressive in establishing a time factor when you originally set the goal and it is not feasible for you to accomplish it in the allotted time. This is a time to just sit down and decide what a more realistic goal is. Remember, one of the elements is that the goal has to be realistic. Your excitement may have coaxed you into setting a goal that was outside of your reach from the beginning.

On the other hand, you may find that the time allotted was not aggressive enough and the target date needs to be shortened. This is why I stress that you have to put a lot of thought into writing these goals. And they do not have to be set during your initial drafting. Write some ideas down and then go back a day or two later and look at them again. Do they still make sense or should they be adjusted. Most likely you will be adjusting them. And these adjustments can be an ongoing strategy.

Not only can the time factors be adjusted but each of the elements can. These goals are for you and you are the only one who knows what is acceptable or not. If you show a stubborn side and refuse to adjust a goal that should be adjusted, you are hurting yourself. There are several reasons goals should be adjusted. Too many other things can happen such as discouragement, injury, and frustration that will cause you to stop trying at all. This is why it is so important to sit down and put considerable thought into establishing your goals. Also, you may accomplish some goals and they will need to be replaced with other goals or just similar goals but more stretching. For example, once you complete the 5K race, then perhaps it is on to the 10K or even the marathon. If you originally established nine months down the road for accomplishing the 5K and it has been only two months, does it make sense that you just keep only running 3 miles when you have a goal in the back of your mind of running a marathon? Probably not, but only you can determine that. Perhaps you are not happy with the time of the 5K and you wish to run it for another 30 days to improve your time, then that is acceptable. Remember, these are your goals and only your goals. You only have to answer to yourself and as long as you are focused and intense about attaining the goal, you are on the right track.

There are several reasons why goals should be adjusted, even down the road. It may just be that you were too aggressive when you first established a particular goal. For example, perhaps you listed losing twenty pounds over a two week period. This result may be possible but not a practical decision and may be harmful to your health. Goals are not a race but a self directed approach to an end result. Maybe you were not aggressive enough in your original goal. You may have stated you wanted to lose twenty pounds over the next six months, but find that you accomplished it in three months. Adjust the goal by increasing the anticipated weight loss, assuming it is your desire to lose more. If not, then change the goal and add a new one. Unforeseeable circumstances may prevent you from attaining the goal. Perhaps a necessary surgery will sideline you from physical activity. Again, listen to the doctor and replace the goal temporarily. Find a goal that would be more realistic such as improving your education or reading. Remember, goals should be never ending. Once you complete one satisfactorily, increase it or replace it. Keep the list ongoing. These goals should help you to develop your inner self.

When you originally sit down to write out the goals, visualize the entire process from how you are going to start out on the goal to actually accomplishing it. This may help you to get a grasp on the plan to accomplish the goal. It may also offer you the opportunity to set other goals that are directly related to the first goal. For example, if you set a goal of running a 5K, had you thought about goals surrounding losing weight, assuming this was necessary? As you write down each goal, you will be surprised of the end result. And I emphasize writing each goal down. It is absolutely imperative that all goals be written. This should be one of the elements of your establishing any goals.

The question comes up as to how long a period it should be in setting goals. There is not solid answer here other than it depends on the goal. You should however have long and short term goals. Running a 5K or losing 10 pounds are short term goals. Attaining your MBA degree when you are only half way through your undergraduate program is a long term goal.

Purchasing 10 rental homes when you have none is a long term goal, in most cases. Set goals for less than one year, one to five years, and goals that will take more than five years. Some of the short term goals will tie into the long term goals and actually may serve as "training times" for the long term goals. Such is the case of purchasing your tenth investment home. Make purchasing your first rental home a short term goal and adding one every six to nine months is not only a short term goal but a long term goal as well. The first home serves as training for purchasing additional homes. Although they all tie in to each other, you are gradually working on attaining your long term goal. You are also able to see progress for your long term goal by attaining these smaller related goals. You will be amazed at how easy the long term goal becomes as you become successful with the short term goals.

At this point, you have enough information to start establishing your goals. As we discussed previously, make sure they are written goals. This helps you in monitoring your results as well as keeping you honest. Visualize yourself accomplishing each goal. This will give you confidence as you tackle the goal. You can keep a hard copy of your goals or you can set up a spreadsheet on your computer. You can even print the spreadsheet out and post it on your wall where you will see it every day.

Below, I have inserted a sample tracking chart that can be set up on your computer. Remember, goals don't work just by writing them down but by following the plan you established for each goal. This is the only way you will succeed.

CATEGORY	GOAL	Sun	Mon	Tue	Wed	Thur	Fri	Sat
SPIRITUAL	5 HRS							
BIBLE	50 PG							
FAMILY TIME	8 HRS							
READING	1 BK.							
CHARITY	2 HRS.							
CAREER GOAL	4 HRS.							
FITNESS	3 HRS.							
EDUCATION	2 HRS.							

"The trouble with not having a goal is that you can spend your life running up and down the field and never score."

-Bill Copeland

11.
JOB ACCEPTANCE

FINALLY, AFTER ALL THOSE LONG HOURS OF NETWORKING AND interviewing, you have landed that perfect job. The phone rang and by the time you actually realized who it was, you were offered a job. You were so excited that you accepted the position before you even had time to realize what the compensation was. Wrong! Of course, there is a tendency to accept the job because it has been a while since you received a paycheck. However, you cannot leave anything on the table in the form of benefits or compensation. Any good recruiter expects you to counteroffer their original offer.

First, you must thank them for the offer but request time to review the offer. Any recruiter that makes a job offer will expect you to request some time to think it over. Obviously you don't want to wait five or six days to get back to them, but it is common to take a day or two to think about the offer. Don't stall it for two days just because that may be expected. If you can come to a conclusion in twenty four hours, then call them back. This is a crucial time, and although it most probably won't be your last job, you must think that it will. You want to make sure the entire compensation package is going to work for you. Look for a win-win situation so that both you and the prospective employer are happy. Remember also, that the one who brings up salary first loses, so let them make the initial offer.

You may initially think it is the salary that should be at the top of the list but this is not always the case. There are other items that must be considered. This is not to say that ultimately the salary will be the key but you have to look at each benefit that the company offers. In some cases, it may be that other benefits are more important to you. For example, I left a position a couple of years ago where my medical insurance cost me $2,400 annually with a $250 deductible to accept a position where the insurance cost me $6,000 annually with a $3,000 deductible. That is a net difference of $6,350 annually. So I had to make up

$6,000 in base salary in order to get ahead of the game. I took this into consideration as I negotiated a final salary, and I got exactly what I wanted.

Let's look at the potential benefits you could receive. Obviously, salary is initially at the top of the list. If the initial offer is $75,000, it is quite possible that the employer has built in some lead way to go higher, such as $80,000 or even $85,000. I have known employers who have had as much as $20,000 available for negotiation. Don't make this decision until you have reviewed each of the other benefits. It may be feasible for you to negotiate salary last. There could quite possibly be other benefits more important to you.

If it is necessary for you to relocate, is the company offering any kind of relocation package? Some companies do not and they usually make that known at the initial interview, whether it was a phone or face to face interview. Relocation can be quite an expensive endeavor and should be approached quite cautiously. It is not just hiring a moving company that is the main expense involved. What if the move requires you to relocate from Florida to Chicago? Think of the expenses that are prevalent in Chicago that were not present in Florida: increased heating costs, possibly higher priced homes, winter clothing, and perhaps even higher property taxes. Maybe your spouse was employed in an industry that pays higher wages in Florida than in Chicago. Will your spouse have to take a reduced salary? Were your in-laws, at no cost, the care takers of your children and now you will have to hire someone to watch over them?

Cost of living varies throughout the United States so you will have to do some investigative work prior to accepting a job offer. At the time you submitted your resume, your investigation should have begun so you have all the details prior to the job offer. Waiting to the last minute only delays or hinders your final decision. Maybe you will find that the increased expenses will be considerably higher than any anticipated salary offer you will receive and it is not necessary to pursue this position. Although the offer is tempting, this is something you cannot go back and change. Also, you do not want to undertake relocation only to find out that the compensation package was not sufficient. The key phrase here is do your research and be happy with the final negotiated package.

Moving companies provide an excellent service and you may not have the time, assistance or ability to do it yourself. If you are single with no dependents and little furniture, then you may be able to do it yourself. However, if a moving company is needed then these fees can range anywhere from $5,000 to $25,000 for the move. Certainly if it is in the $25,000 range you do not want to have to pay that out of your pocket, but do not reject a job offer if there is no relocation package until you put the numbers in the calculator. The company may not offer relocation packages but may be willing to increase the salary offer by $10,000. If the move is going to cost you $12,000 and you have to pay that out of your pocket but your salary will be $10,000 higher, this is only a $2,000 difference and that is for the first year. If you anticipate staying with this company for 3, 4 or 5 years, then you are well ahead of the game. The downside is that maybe you do not have $12,000 in cash available for the move. The company may be willing to advance you the relocation costs with a flexible payment plan. Again, look at all sides of it.

It is necessary to point out that many relocation expenses are tax deductible and you should consult an accountant or the IRS to get full details. Obviously, if you are being reimbursed for some of these expenses by your new employer, you cannot claim them on your taxes. Review IRS publication 521 for more details.

If relocation is necessary, will the company pay for you to fly back home on weekends to be with your family until the move is complete? Will they pay for your spouse to fly up on weekends? Will they provide lodging for you and how long if so? Will this include all meals? Many times a company will grant these options. On one move that I made, the company allowed me to fly home every weekend because it was less expensive to do that than put me up in a hotel for three extra nights, as well as the meal costs. Due to my work load, it was not feasible to fly home every weekend but I did fly home every other weekend.

Tuition reimbursement is a benefit most companies provide now. If you have intentions of pursuing an advanced degree such as an MBA, this can run in the vicinity of $10-20,000 in tuition costs. The Masters program at the University of Florida for 2008 is approximately $9,500, not including books. Many times a company will only allow a certain amount such as $5,000 annually, so take this into consideration. What if the company only allows $5,000 maximum, which still may leave a remainder of $15,000 to be paid out of your pocket? This may be an opportunity to negotiate a larger tuition reimbursement. The company may be willing to increase the amount to get you on board. Remember, most benefits are negotiable and not always written in stone.

Company vehicles are common for many positions. This has always been a major benefit to those receiving one, and more so in these times of such high fuel prices with no end in sight. Let us take a look at this in more detail. If you purchase a new vehicle which will be used in your new position, look at what expenses are involved:New automobile purchased for $25,000 less the $5,000 initial down payment. This will result in the financing of $20,000. Using an 8% interest rate for the $20,000, your monthly loan payment will be $488.26 each month for the next 48 months. If we add full auto insurance coverage, your annual cost will probably be in the $1,500 range or $125 per month. Based on gas prices as of April, 2008 ($3.25), for 15, 000 miles at 25 mpg, your fuel cost will be $1,950. Oil changes at 3000 miles will cost you in the vicinity of $200 annually.

Now, let us put these figures to the calculator annualizing each:

Loan payments	$5,859
Auto insurance	$1,500
Fuel costs	$1,950
Oil changes	$200
Total annual costs	$9,459

Keep in mind we did not allow for any maintenance items such as tires, alignments, etc. Let's look at it another way. IRS uses 55.0 cents per mile for tax calculations. Using 55.0 times 15,000 miles, this will result in an annual figure of $8,250, slightly lower than actual annual cost of operating a vehicle. Either way, at the very least you benefit by a minimum of over $8,000 per year by receiving a company vehicle so if you receive an offer of $5,000 less than you wanted yet you get a company car, you are considerably ahead of the game.

Vacation time is one of the more popular benefits. A company usually offers two weeks of vacation after one year yet I have worked for companies that offered as little as one week and as much as three weeks after the first year. In a couple of cases, vacation time can be taken after six months of service. However, this benefit can also be negotiated. Perhaps you can negotiate for one extra week annually. Although it does not directly put money in your pocket, it is a benefit and this is valuable time that can be spent with your family or just used toward a hobby you have or even toward a hobby that you use to produce income. Again, look at each benefit and see how it can affect you in a positive or negative way.

There are many benefits out there. Short and long term disability insurance, cafeteria plans, company sponsored training programs taken off site, on site fitness centers (usually costing you $50 per month or more), and on site cafeterias. Now, some of these benefits are firm and cannot be negotiated but look for those that can. You obviously cannot negotiate fees for fitness centers if the company provides free usage, but if you are paying $50 per month, this annualizes to $600. On site cafeterias usually provide employees with less expensive meals versus going to the local Denny's or even McDonalds. Add these savings up over 50 work weeks. The average employee works 260 days and if you can save just $2.00 per day, that annualizes out to over a $500 savings, to include money you may save on the free coffee the company offers. You are probably sitting there thinking that a $500 savings over twelve months is nothing to get excited about, but start adding all of these savings up. This $500 savings will pay approximately 4 months of your auto insurance, 3 months of fuel for your vehicle, or two or more weeks of your food bill. You can purchase a computer for not much more than this $500 savings. It is better to look at this savings as to what you can do with it versus thinking it is just "a drop in the bucket."

Many times a company will negotiate additional vacation time for employees. Perhaps a new employee normally gets 1 week and you can negotiate a second week or a third week if necessary. The company may have rigid restrictions on the other benefits or even salary, so this provides them a negotiating option in order to hire the desired individual. The opportunity also exists to negotiate additional personal days or even paid leave time to complete the relocation. I remember one situation where a company granted long weekends every other weekend for an employee to travel home. This allowed him time to spend with his family, especially where he was away two weeks at a time.

As you can see from the different scenarios here that many organizations will be open to negotiation. They have spent thousands of dollars to locate the ideal candidate and they certainly do not want to lose that candidate for a few hundred dollars more. They may have arrangements with independent recruiters to locate a candidate and if their final decision results in a candidate who was not recruited through an outside agency, then this savings of thousands of dollars results in them having the resources to offer additional benefits to the potential candidate. Keep this in mind before you accept any offer. Was the position listed with a recruiter and you were offered the position through your own efforts? A newly hired employee with a salary of $100,000 can cost a company anywhere from $20-40,000. You can use this to your advantage and don't be afraid to state your knowledge of this. Obviously you do not know what their agreement with the outside agency is, but rest assured it is 20-40 % of the total salary.

Once you have finalized an offer, then is the time to start everything else rolling. Offer a two week notice to your current employer if you have one. I stress this because you may have to come back to them some day for a position if the current one does not work out. And once you submit your notice, do not sit back on your laurels. Just recently a friend of mine accepted a position in another state and just two days before he was to leave, the new company contacted him and rescinded their offer without stating a reason. Although he was unemployed at the time, had he been employed and offered his letter of resignation and maintained a satisfactory work record, most likely he could have stayed on board. But what if he had not maintained a good record; do you think the current company would allow him to stay on board? Probably not, so keep that line of communication open.

As you wind down your final period of resignation, ensure that you have completed all projects and assignments that were given to you. Just because you are leaving in two weeks and you may not see the end result of what you were working on, don't drop the ball. You arrived at your current company with your integrity, so make sure you leave with it. Too often employees submit their resignation and decide to just take a two week vacation by showing up every day, or in many cases they take numerous unjustified sick days because these days "are due them." This is a bad attitude and not one you want to take with you.

Whether you feel your current company treated you right or not, you have no reason to show a lack of integrity or remorse, nor do you have the right to steal from the company. Showing up every day and sitting with your legs up on the desk is stealing, just as it would be if you absconded with items from your desk. You are being paid by the company for accomplishing certain tasks. There was never anything in your original agreement where once you submitted a resignation that you could just take it easy for two weeks. If the company treated you fairly, then return the favor. If they treated you unfairly, don't play their game. As stated previously, you never know when you may need to be rehired. Or what if the new company you go to work for is merged with your current company and positions need to be eliminated. Dare I say who would be on the top of that list? Just continue on as if it were another day and just count down the days to your new starting date.

If you were not employed when you accepted the new position, then perhaps you can start the new job immediately. The time you recently had off work looking for a new position was sufficient time out of work. You don't need a vacation now. Start off on the right foot and ask them how soon you may be able to start. That shows your eagerness and willingness to be part of your new team. Perhaps the position is not available for two weeks and your starting date will be delayed due to this reason. Take this time and prepare yourself for the new job, at the same time complete any pending projects around the house. You will find with your new found attitude, these projects will be more pleasant and enjoyable. If funds permit it, take a couple of days and get away to relax. It may be awhile before you will have a vacation.

What I would further suggest is that once you know your new compensation package, request it in writing from the hiring party. Most companies automatically do this now, but you will feel more secure with this letter and less chance that when you get on board, there are no surprises. There are cases where an offer has been made by the hiring party of the new company and you get on board only to find out that party is no longer with the company and the offer made to you was out of his authority to offer. With the signed offer, the company will more likely be willing to stand behind it and not doubt your word of the offer.

Now is the time to make sure everything is ready to go for the first day of work. Get that shirt pressed, the shoes polished and put lead in the pencil. You are off on a new career/position that hopefully will bring you much success.

"A winner is someone who recognizes his God given talents, works his tail off to develop them into skills, and uses these skills to accomplish his goals."

-Larry Bird

12.
PUTTING IT ALL TOGETHER

LET'S STEP BACK AND REVIEW ALL THAT YOU HAVE READ ABOUT locating a new position. We have discussed downsizing and the effects it can have on you. It causes stress, rage, anger, depression, marital, and financial problems. From the day you receive the notification of your termination, your comfort zone has been turned upside down. After you get over that initial shock, put your positive mental attitude hat on and start out on your search. Keep the thought close to you that this is the beginning of a new, great chapter in your life. Letting yourself get wrapped up in all the negativity that will surround you only brings you down and seriously hampers your search.

If you do not have a fitness routine, get it started now and commit to it. Set it up to work three or four times per week. Make it a fun time and create the attitude that you look forward to it. Sitting around or as the saying goes, becoming a "couch potato" will only provide food for depression. If you have a gym membership, continue using it or if no membership, then look into facilities at your subdivisions clubhouse. If funds prevent you from joining a fitness center, there are many things you can do at home. For weights, venture to the garage and locate a five gallon can of paint. That will provide a good start to a weight program. Most department stores have small hand weights that you can purchase for $7 or $8. Do your children have a jump rope that you can use? And of course, walking provides a free exercise. Look for any opportunity to exercise as this will serve to lower your stress level.

Create a checklist, if necessary to get the ball rolling. As we discussed previously, contact your local unemployment office immediately and get those benefits started. Most likely you will qualify for assistance, so take advantage of it. Start by going on the Internet and begin your research there. You will have no problem locating an office close by, but you should not have to even visit the office initially. Once your claim has been approved they may call you in to advise you of what services they offer. Many offices offer job training assistance such as free courses. These range from computer courses to retraining to move you into a new occupation. The next step should be to follow up on your COBRA. You have to continue health insurance coverage and you will only have a fixed amount of time to enroll.

Get started on creating that management team. Make sure your family, friends, church partners, neighbors, and former employers or employees know your status. Any one of them could offer you some valid leads or suggestions. Set up an immediate schedule with your team, either one on one or all together. Some of them may have been in the same situation as you currently are and can direct you to some great resources. Don't forget to sit down with your family and explain the situation to them. I remember one friend who lost his job and his teenage son offered to eliminate his weekly allowance. Give your family the opportunity to be part of it. You may find they are more compassionate than you realized.

Set up your answering machine with an appropriate professional message. Make sure there is pen and paper next to the phone for any messages that your family may take. Explain to each of them how important it is to get detailed messages. You certainly do not want to lose any messages that could lead you to your next position. And don't forget to check your machine throughout the day when you are out on the road. You may receive a phone call from someone that wants to see you as soon as possible, and you just passed their office.

Along with your fitness routine, make sure you maintain a proper diet. Getting all wrapped up in your job search tends to have you forget to eat. Don't skip meals and avoid those fast food restaurants. First, because they are costly and second, they do not provide your daily dietary requirements. Now you may find yourself on the road all day and if you are not able to bring along a cooler with a sandwich, you might find it necessary to stop for lunch. Do not skip lunch under any circumstances.

As you are working out your plan, consider if this is an appropriate time to change careers. Take some skill assessments and determine if a change in career is best for you. My career began in the financial services industry and after going thru several company mergers, three in one ninety day period, I decided to take my qualifications and change directions. It provided me with a whole new direction and of course, a job that came about quicker than if I had stayed in my previous occupation. It never hurts to find out who you really are and this is an excellent time to accomplish that. As you come to this conclusion or even during the process, set some new goals. These goals could tie into what direction you want to take. They will also assist you in establishing that direction with a roadmap. Use the SMART method which we discussed in the first chapter. These goals must be specific, measurable, attainable, realistic, and of course, time bound.

Don't think for a minute that this time in your life is going to be a joy nor a disaster. Approach it as just another chapter. Locating that next job is going to be a job and you will probably work harder than some of your past jobs. It is a changing world out there and the way you found jobs five or ten years ago may not work any longer. In fact, some of the positions you have held may not even be realistic any longer. The job market has become quite duty specific. Let's take for example the IT world. Just stating you are an IT professional does not say anything at all. In the past you may have done some programming and worked a help desk, among other duties. Each of these tasks is a now full time job in itself. You may need some additional training or certifications so what better time to update your qualifications. Look into continuing education courses and get any necessary certifications. They will only make your resume look that much stronger.

Let's get back to some basics in your search preparation. Set up your office accordingly. Is your resume up to date? Do you have sufficient copies printed? Take your briefcase out of mothballs and prepare it for your search process. Get some business cards printed and make sure they are professional looking. Keep a supply on you at all times. You never know when the opportunity may arise that you need to pass one on. It could happen when you scurry down to the local convenience store at 11:00 p.m. There should be a couple kept in your wallet for these particular times. Of course, always bring a sufficient supply with you when you leave your home each day. Name tags should be professional as well. Both name tags and business cards can be printed right on your home computer for just a few dollars. Along with updating your resume, get your Marketing Plan ready as well. You want to be fully prepared when you take that first step out the door on your new search.

The first couple of days in your new search can be spent on establishing a list of networking opportunities. Refer back to the list in chapter one and develop your own list of names that you want to contact. Do not leave anyone out as that is the person who could possibly help you the most. You won't know when or where that great opportunity will arise so make every attempt to generate the possibility. It could be the Pastor of your church or the gentleman next to you on the treadmill at the local YMCA.

During your planning and researching stage, create the Mission and Vision Statements in accordance with your goals. You will find during this process that you may not have been traveling the career road that is suitable for you. Remember, both of these should be completed in privacy and not with your management team. Once you have all your notes together, then perhaps you can consult with your team, but the mind will produce more intelligent thoughts if you are not sitting in the middle of Shea Stadium. The beach, a quiet spot in the corner of your backyard, the den with the door locked, or perhaps a quiet ride in the country. The ride will prevent you from doing any writing but carry a tape recorder with you for your thoughts.

As you go along, your original version will need some editing. Your goals may change or you may just choose a new direction in life. Maybe you were employed in corporate America but now you choose a more spiritual direction. These instances can greatly change not only your goals but your outlook on life. Don't hesitate to adjust your Mission and Vision Statements but of course, not weekly. Changing it as often as once a week or once a month will not give you strong direction. Make sure you have covered what you are truly passionate about.

Throughout your job search process, it is imperative that your faith and spiritual well being be at the top of your list. Attending church regularly will ease some of the burden. If your church offers daily Mass, take advantage of it. You will find your attitude will adjust itself and your outlook on life will greatly improve, even under these circumstances. You should not waiver in your faith in that the Lord will bring you through this period of calamity. Not only will you see your attitude stay strong but your self-esteem will also hold strong. Take every opportunity to get to know God and thank him for what He has done for you and your family. Praise Him daily.

As you plan your method of attack, spend time reviewing your financial situation. Take account of what your assets and liabilities are. Look over your assets and determine your available cash and how long it will last you. Can you reduce any of your daily expenses? Look for coupons in the newspaper and don't feel awkward using them. Can you visit the local Goodwill or Salvation Army store? Eliminate the lawn and pool care until you are back to work. This could save you hundreds of dollars monthly. Are you able to perform any temporary work that will help with some of the expenses? Create a new budget based on your current financial situation. Include the funds you will receive from unemployment compensation, welfare, food stamps, severance packages and any other income than comes into the household.

Change your buying habits and look to getting the most for your money. Avoid the upscale department stores such as J.C. Penney, Sears, or Macy's. Shop at Wal-Mart and Kmart, or other discount stores. Speak to your Pastor for any assistance that may be available from your church. Look into getting any help with your charge cards and mortgage companies. They may have temporary programs to get you through this period of adjustment. You want to do everything possible to avoid bankruptcy.

As you dust off your old resume, take time to make notes on it and adjust it since you originally created it. Remember, this is your gift wrap and what will get you those interviews. Do not fabricate any part of it at all. Lying on your resume will eventually cause you more grief. Review the newly created resume several times to insure you have all of your "wows" listed. Don't make it more than two pages long and be certain to use spell check. It is embarrassing to be sitting in an interview and the recruiter notice you spelled something wrong. Remember, you do have the option of using a professional resume writing company but there will be a substantial cost involved in doing this.

Before you complete the resume, you will have to decide whether the functional or chronological resume best suits your needs. If you have had several jobs recently, then the functional resume will be your best bet. If your job history is solid, then go with the chronological. You can always use a combined functional-chronological resume if in doubt. Don't be afraid to brag a little, but do remember that bragging is alright but arrogance is not acceptable. Once the resume is complete, get it posted on any Internet sites that cater to your profession. Obviously, Monster and CareerBuilder are definite possibilities. If you are in accounting, look for those sites that cater to the accounting profession. The banking industry has several of their own, as well as the call center industry.

Now that you have everything ready, get out and do some networking. Review the list that you prepared of possible sources and get on the phone and out in the public. Networking is a game of numbers and the more people you make contact with, the greater the opportunity of landing a job quickly. Develop a list of people of influence that can act as your "look-outs." Establish some weekly networking goals and adjust them accordingly. Networking can best be accomplished by visiting local meetings and events, some during the day and some held after dinner. Find the ones that are going to provide you with the most benefit. Visiting the local wine tasting party and avoiding a career search group won't accomplish your goal.

As you attend these networking events, don't make it just a numbers game. Make each contact count and if it proves that it will not be a good contact, move on to the next one. Wear your name tag and have an ample supply of business cards in your pocket. Do not get them mixed up with the cards you will be collecting. It will be unfortunate to pass out a card that you received from the last contact in place of yours. Put the business cards you collected in a different pocket than yours. When you meet these contacts, shake their hand and maintain a positive attitude. They don't want you crying on their shoulder as they may be in the same situation as you. As you collect these business cards, jot something down on the back to signify an item that you want to remember about them. It will prove beneficial days or weeks down the road when you meet them again.

Make every attempt to meet three or four solid contacts at each event. Although we keep mentioning a numbers game, this is not the time to worry about that. Look for contacts that not only can help you but that you may be able to help as well. They will be more open to helping you if they realize you will help them. Do not ask any of the contacts that you met where you can locate a job. At best, let them know you are a transitioning professional and they will understand your intentions. And any contact you meet, make sure you send them a thank you email and follow up with them occasionally. Continue to work each lead you developed.

Statistics show that most positions are obtained through networking and my experience further justifies this. It is estimated that around 75% of most professional positions are located by solid networking efforts. However, you must use every source available to you and the Internet is a viable source. Many people have secured great positions through their Internet search. Take advantage of any website that caters to your profession. As we discussed previously, Monster and Career Builder are two of the largest on the web. Not only can you use the Internet to locate a position but you can research most companies as well. Prior to an interview use this source to locate what you can about your prospective employer. Make sure your resume is posted on every available site, but again beware, that many marketing companies use this to develop leads. You will most definitely receive daily emails from prescription drug companies to online dating firms. Another source on the Internet is job alerts. Monster and CareerBuilder allow you to post alerts for positions that match certain criteria. You can get these daily or weekly and the cost is free. You can also set up Google alerts that will keep you advised of events or press releases in your field.

Headhunters, recruiters, employment agencies and career firms are other sources to get the word out to organizations that you are in the hunt. There are several good books at your local library that will direct you to a specific company that specializes in your profession. For example, if you are in banking, there are recruiters that only deal with the banking industry. They have made hundreds of contacts at the senior level and know how to get your resume in the door. This is also a good opportunity to have someone else "sell you" and just maybe a new position can be created for someone with your talents and skills. They are able to build strong, long-term relationships with many centers of influence in your target organizations.

One of the larger chapters in this book covered interviewing. Although there is no fool proof way to score a hit on an interview, knowing all of the basics will at least keep you deep in the hunt. But your success will depend on how well you prepare, whether it be for the behavioral, functional, or informational interview. It is more difficult to prepare for the behavioral due to the complexity of the questions that are asked, but with preparation and practice, you can come out with flying colors. Keep in the mind the SAR method we discussed in the interviewing chapter. When you are presented with a question, first reply with the situation, then the action you took and lastly the results that were obtained.

First impressions are lasting impressions and within the first 10 seconds you walk into an interview, an impression has been made. Having on a nicely pressed suit or other outfit and polished shoes gives you a good start. Keep the cologne and perfume to a minimum, and avoid it if possible. Your fragrance may not wear so well on the other person. Haven't you ever sat next to someone on an airplane or even in church and the odor totally took your concentration away? Keep the flashy pins and purses back at home. No "wild and crazy" guys here, as the famed actor Steve Martin stated. Make sure the hair is neat and the fingernails well manicured.

Practice your presentation and then practice it again, and then practice it one more time. You cannot get too much practice. Obtaining this position could depend on how well prepared you are. Even if it is a telephone interview, go ahead and get dressed up. You will feel better and that will show through on the telephone. Make dry runs to the interview the day before at the same time of your scheduled interview. This allows you sufficient knowledge of the traffic flow and how much time you will need. Late arrivals will be at a disadvantage once they walk into the interview room. Arrive early and use the rest room to touch up that strand of hair that just won't cooperate with you today.

During your interview process make sure you shake the interviewers hand and smile throughout the visit. Show appropriate body language and avoid any disturbing habits such as clicking pens or playing with your hair. When you sit down, place yourself as far back in the chair as possible and this will help you to align yourself. If it is a luncheon interview, watch your eating habits. Do not think for a moment that they will take their eyes off of you. If you are interviewing for a sales position, they will especially be watching how you would handle yourself with a client. Avoid any foods that could cause hazards such as pasta sauces, spare ribs, etc. You get the idea of what not to order and let your host order first and follow their lead. If they order a sandwich, then go that route. You do not want to be embarrassed ordering a thick steak and all they end up ordering is a salad. Of course if you are on special diets due to a health condition don't vary and take an appropriate opportunity to mention it in passing. Your host will understand. And lastly, avoid alcohol or "truth serum" as I like to say.

Just because it is a relaxed lunch, don't think that the interview has not started. Most of their questions will have some relationship to the position you are seeking. Take your time to think about your answers before giving them. Speak slowly but confidently and this will serve as a reassurance to them of the person they are looking to hire. Same thing goes for any salary discussions, think before you reply and don't answer too hastily. And lastly, as you get up to leave make sure you thank them for the interview and follow it up with a mailed thank you note. Once you leave the interview, take a few minutes and sit in your automobile and critique how you handled the interview. This will help you to prepare for the next interview.

During your career search it is important to stay positive and motivated. Eliminate any negative thoughts that cross your mind. Look for the positives in everything that you say and do. One way is to listen to motivational speakers as you drive around. Most of the top motivational speakers in the world have CD's or even cassettes recorded that you can either purchase or obtain through your local library. Go to the library website and search speakers such as Zig Ziglar, Denis Waitley, Anthony Robbins or Napoleon Hill. You will reap many rewards from listening to these CD's or even reading their books.

Decided to take the leap into entrepreneurship? Then, just as you had done during your job search process, make sure you research it to its fullest. Think hard before you make any decisions and consult as many experts in the field as possible. This goes anywhere from your accountant to the SBA. Look at not only the financial side of owning your own business but the emotional side as well. Remember, going into business is not a way to semi-retire. You may find yourself working harder than any job you held in the past. The plus side is that having your own business can be very rewarding, not only financially but emotionally as well. It could provide you with confidence in yourself that you did not know existed. And in the long run, it could provide you with more financial security than you thought possible.

We touched on goals previously and it cannot be stated enough that goals are a vital part to your everyday life, career, family, physical and spiritual well being. Having goals keeps you focused and on track for bigger and better things. They have to become a necessary part of your daily life. Use the SMART method…specific, measurable, actionable, realistic and time bound. Cover every area of your life and adjust them as necessary. Look for areas that you want to improve in. Goals have to be not only short term but long term as well. Remember to break them down in immediate goals (up to 1 year), short term

(1-2 years), mid range (2-5 years) and long term (more than 5 years).

You've been offered the position and your jubilation is through the roof. Pull the reins in and compose yourself because the negotiation period has just started. Make sure before you accept the salary that everything else falls into place. Is the entire benefit package what you are looking for? Do you have to relocate and if so, have you done your research? Cost of living in the new area, prices of homes, cost of the move, are there good schools nearby, and will your spouse be able to find a position in their field with a comparable salary? Is there a relocation package included and is it sufficient to cover all the new expenses? Your research should have been completed prior to the offer, preferably just before the interview. This allows you to focus on last minute details.

Do your due diligence in every area that will affect the new position. Don't overlook any detail to include the health insurance package. Maybe a member of your family has certain medical issues that require a good insurance plan. As you well know the cost of medical procedures continue to rise and just basic surgical procedures can run in the thousands of dollars. Does the plan provide satisfactory deductibles along with premiums? Whether your children are in public or private schools, are there good schools in the area? Are you or your spouse enrolled in continuing education and if so, are there colleges close by? As you can see there are many details that you must research before you accept that offer.

Alright, the benefit package meets your needs and expectations so now what do you do? Take some time and create a letter of resignation offering sufficient time to the current employer, if you are working. In your letter praise the company for what they have given you and how you have benefited from your employment with them. This is important because you never want to leave any burning bridges behind. There may come a time when you may have to return there and if you leave providing them with some kind and appreciative words, chances are greater you will not have a problem in the future. Earlier in my career I worked for a company for four years before leaving for another opportunity. More than twenty years later I had an opportunity to return to another division of that same company and it worked out well. You may think that twenty years down the road no one will remember that far back but in my case, there were several employees that had in excess of thirty years with the company.

There is an online networking service that must not be overlooked. It is www.Linkedin.com and is becoming a valuable asset worldwide. The concept behind it is to bring together people throughout the world. It is free for the basic service, although you may expand the options for a modest fee. When you initially sign on, you create a personal profile that is available to all who visit the site. The profile will include the area of the country or world you are in, current and past employers, education, and your industry. The system will track those others who have affiliations with your current and past employers, giving you the opportunity to network with them. It is based on the degrees of contact. For example, if you and I were friends and connected on Linkedin, we would be level 1 contacts. Any of your contacts would then become my level 2 contacts and vice versa. Any contacts belonging to your contacts would be level 3 contacts. The premise is that you are connected indirectly to those other contacts and could request the assistance of your immediate contract for an introduction. As of the writing of this book, if you had 80 contacts, then you have access indirectly to approximately 1.7 million others, and 200 contacts upwards to over 5 million.

Also on the Linkedin site you are able to search for available positions based on zip codes. Should you see a position that interests you, the site will indicate whether you have any contacts affiliated with the company along with their name. So for example, let's say XYZ Corporation had a position for an IT Engineer posted and the hiring manager was a level 2 contact. Once you view how that hiring manager is connected to you, you would simply contact your level 1 contact and request an introduction. Also on the site there are questions posted by the members on a daily basis requesting your input, if you so desire. You have the opportunity to answer the question and form some credibility in this area of expertise. One other good benefit of Linkedin is that you can become a member of certain groups where you are able to network with that particular group. For example if you are a member of the North American Call Center Professionals group, you can network with other call center professionals. Take advantage of this free service.

You have submitted your resignation and now you can just sit back and relax. These words are so far from the truth! It is your obligation to continue to provide your existing company with your best efforts. First of all, keep in mind that the new job offer can be rescinded without cause. Second, your integrity should never be questioned. Don't feel you can now take advantage of that unused sick time or plod along as if you had nowhere to go. Leave at the end of your resignation period with your head held high and a sense of satisfaction that you accomplished everything necessary to leave your replacement with a good start. And if the new position involves relocation, you have many things to take care of in preparation for the move. You may find that you will be working harder over the next two weeks than prior to giving your resignation. Be excited over the new position but be focused on the task at hand.

We sincerely hope that this book has provided you with some basic understanding of the job search. It is a trying time, whether you are employed or not. If you stay focused and committed to finding that perfect career position, half the battle is over. Good luck in your search and remember the following:

"I am the master of my fate and the captain of my soul."
-William Ernest Henley

HAVE YOU...

1. Reviewed your severance package? _____
2. Reviewed your Outlook contacts? _____
3. Obtained reference letters from co-workers, boss, etc? _____
4. Filed your unemployment compensation claim? _____
5. Had a family meeting to explain situation? _____
6. Established your COBRA benefits? _____
7. Set up a fitness program? _____
8. Obtained a copy of your credit report? _____
9. Set up your management team and mentor? _____
10. Set up a proper answering machine message? _____
11. Set up your office and briefcase? _____
12. Established a professional email address? _____
13. Developed a job search plan/strategy? _____
14. Had a skills assessment completed? _____
15. Updated or created a resume? _____
16. Created a Marketing Plan? _____
17. Created your Mission & Vision Statements? _____
18. Established goals? _____
19. Contacted family and friends? _____
20. Created an elevator speech? _____
21. Established personal and family time? _____
22. Contacted your Pastor? _____
23. Reviewed your assets, liabilities & budget? _____

24. Established a "panic" date? _____

25. Obtained IRS publications? _____

26. Had business cards printed? _____

27. Created a name tag? _____

28. Created job alerts on Internet websites? _____

29. Volunteered in church and community? _____

30. Established prayer time? _____

31. Attended church? _____

32. Updated your educational skills? _____

33. Created a profile on Linkedin? _____

34. Contacted recruiters in your occupational field? _____

35. Networked, Networked, Networked? _____

INDEX

Action Verbs, 62
Alimony, 49
Alumni, 94
Anger, 1, 9, 166
Appearance, 119, 9
Assessments, 14-15, 167
Assets, 18, 48, 51, 170
Baber, Anne, 96
Baby Boomers, 111
Bacon, Kevin, 92
Bankruptcy, 5, 58
Baskin Robbins, 40
Benefits, 158-163, 176
Bible, 43-45
Bird, Larry, 165
Blanchard, Ken, 150
Book of Lists, 76
Bossidy, Larry, 107
Budgets, 47, 50
Bureau of Labor Statistics, 43
Business cards, 21, 96-97, 99, 101, 168
Calendars, 29-31, 79, 103
CareerBuilder, 108, 172
Charge/credit cards, 54, 170
Child care, 49
COBRA, 7-8, 51-52, 167
Confidence, 13, 15, 44, 93, 96, 103, 117, 127-128, 136, 138-139, 156, 175
Consulting, 52
Consumer Credit Counseling, 57
Copeland, Bill, 157
Cover letters, 78
Covey, Stephen, 29, 37
Credit Reports, 6, 58
Deductions, 54-56
Dell, 13
Department of Labor, 52
Depression, 166
Discrimination, 9, 71
Downsizing, 1

Drake, Bean, Morin, 6
Edison, Thomas, 143
Education, 19-20
EEOC, 9, 134
Elevator speech, 98-99, 135-136
Email, 67, 75-76
Employment agencies, 173
Entrepreneurship, 144-148
Exercise, 3-4, 12-13
Faith, 2, 19, 37, 42
Finances, 4758
Fisher, Donna, 96
Fonts, 60
Franchises, 147
Gandhi, Mahatma, 116
Gatekeepers, 100, 122
General Electric, 13
General Motors, 39-40
Gide, Andre, 148
Goals, 15-18, 149-157, 175-176
God, 42-46, 170
Goodwill Store, 53, 170
Google, 67, 110, 122, 125
Government assistance, 51
Hahn, Kurt, 41
Handshaking, 96, 127
Harrison, Joe, 33
Health insurance, 8, 166-167, 176
HELOC, 5, 56-57
Henley, William, 178
Hill, Napoleon, 29, 175
Illegal questions, 135
Internet, 108-110
Interviews, 117-143, 173-174
  Behavioral, 118
  Functional, 119
IRS forms/publications, 48, 54-56
J.C. Penney, 53, 170
Job fairs, 100-101
Kmart, 13, 53, 170
Liabilities, 48, 51
Linkedin, 107, 114-115, 177

Lombardi, Vince, 32
Macy's, 53, 170
Malcolm X, 79
Market Plans, 23-27
Mergers, 1
Mission Statement, 34-40, 169
Monster, 108, 172
Mortgage payments, 56
Name tags, 21, 97, 169
Networking, 28, 93-107, 169, 171
Nightingale-Conant, 39
Outlook, 30-31
Outsourcing, 1
Panic Date, 41
Pastor, 11, 44, 170
Princeton Review, 14
Recession, 3
Recruiters, 58, 111-114, 173
Relocation packages, 158-163, 176
Restructures, 1
Resumes, 58-171
Resume Blasting, 63
Rightsizing, 1
Robbins, Anthony, 29, 175
St. Augustine, 46
S.A.R., 118, 130-131, 173
S.C.O.R.E., 145
S.M.A.R.T., 17, 150-151, 168, 175
S.T.A.R., 131

Salary.com, 139
Salary negotiations, 76, 139-142, 158
Salvation Army, 53, 170
SBA, 175
Schwab, Charles, 58
Sears, 53, 170
Self-esteem, 44
Severance package, 7
Six Degrees of Separation, 92, 95, 114
Spell check, 60
Spiritual, 42-46
Sprint, 40
Thank you letters, 12, 21, 99, 107, 122, 142, 172, 175
Toastmasters, 39, 41
Tuition, 150
Unemployment compensation, 8, 22, 47
Vilas, Sandy, 96
Vision Statements, 34, 40-41, 169
VistaPrint, 41
Voicemail, 10-11, 167
Waitley, Denis, 29, 151, 175
Walmart, 53, 170
Waymon, Lynne, 96
YMCA, 3, 169
Ziglar, Zig, 29, 175